THE KIMMY DIARIES

The diary of a very spoilt cat

BY KIMMY

Authors On Line

Visit us online at www.authorsonline.co.uk

An Authors OnLine Book

ISBN 978-07552-0436-6

Authors OnLine Ltd
19 The Cinques
Gamlingay, Sandy
Bedfordshire SG19 3NU
England

This book is also available in e-book format, details of which are available at www.authorsonline.co.uk

Dedications

To all the cats and dogs and small animals at Bath Cats and Dogs Home and to everyone who works there – from Kimmy with gratitude.

Useful Contacts

www.Bathcatsanddogshome.co.uk
www.petethevet.com
www.rspca.org.uk
Pete.Wedderburn@telegraph.co.uk

Foreword

As I write this, I have yet to meet Kimmy in person. I first heard about her when Christine sent me an email with a question for my weekly Daily Telegraph column. At the time, she had queries about Kimmy's diet, as you can read if you turn to chapter 19. When I heard that Kimmy had put paw to paper to write her own book, I was more than happy to help out, especially since the project is a fund-raiser for a good cause.

Bath Cats and Dogs Home carry out immensely valuable work for less fortunate animals, as do many other animal rescue centres across the United Kingdom. Most of the work is done by volunteers, but the financial cost of caring for the animals is high. Fundraising is a continual challenge. Many people enjoy giving up their time to work with the animals, but it feels less rewarding to shake a collecting can or write to businesses looking for funds. It's great that Kimmy has taken the initiative to raise money in a different, fun way.

There are so many unwanted animals, and it is always heart-warming to hear when an animal finds a good home. Kimmy is a good example of how well things can turn out, but there are thousands of cats like Kimmy who may never find the home that they need. (Well…. Perhaps not quite like her). Animal rescue centres like Bath Cats and Dogs Home need the ongoing support of the communities around them. If we all work together, we can maximise the chances of unwanted cats and dogs finding the comfortable niche in life that they deserve.

Pets are good for people. They bring so many pleasures into our lives. The exhilaration of seeing a dog enjoy a long country walk on a clear day. The comfort of having a contented, purring cat sitting on your lap. A pet doesn't need to be as spoilt as Kimmy to have a good life – enough food, decent shelter, and some daily attention is all that is needed if you are thinking of giving a home to an animal.

Thank you for buying this book, and I trust you will enjoy reading Kimmy's miaowings and purrs. Do remember to include your local animal rescue centre in your life. If you live near Bath, contact Bath Cats and Dogs Home and see if you can help in any way. If you live elsewhere, ask around and find out who needs help. If we all do a small bit, it makes it easier to accomplish the huge job that needs to be done on behalf of the unwanted animals in the world.

Pete Wedderburn BVM&S CertVR MRCVS

Chapter One

The Home

Wednesday 16th May

I, Kimmy, dreamt that I was sleeping on a huge comfy armchair by a roaring fire but instead I woke up in the same open-prison I'd been in for months now. An empty bowl lay in front of me - my little pink and green blanket covered the crumbs of food that I'd left and an ugly ginger tom was scowling through the bars at me from the next cage. I tried to be brave and not cry.

My life hadn't always been like this. Once I had a good home in a tidy little bungalow with a grey haired lady who loved and cared for me. One day she bundled me into a basket and took me to this big place, full of noisy cats and dogs - and some chickens too I was told. She left me here saying she was moving into one of those homes for old people only and couldn't take me. Why not? Am I not old enough? It sounded a lot like here only for humans instead of animals. Why couldn't I go with her? I liked old people. I am only small and don't take up much room - they'd hardly notice me. But instead I was dumped in the cage that's been mine for the past three months. I knew it was that long because I heard Louise, one of my carers saying,

'I can't believe that Kimmy has been here for three months now when she is so gorgeous'.

Did I mention that I am gorgeous? Well, believe me I am. I am a beautiful tabby with a white bib and face.

Louise was one of the people who fed me and cleaned out my litter tray. I'd had to learn how to use one of those because I hadn't had one at my old house. Jack was the other one who looked after me. He was always joking and despite him not taking me home to sleep on his bed, he was lovely. Sometimes he sneaked me a little extra Whiskas and Louise often picked me up and hugged me. Jack said he was not supposed to have favourites (why not?) but if he did I would be his.

Now Louise was banging around outside my cage as she began to give us all our breakfast. There were about thirty of us in our block which was called the 'New' Cattery. We had an outside garden view as opposed to the other blocks that didn't look out on anything much. I heard there were dozens of us here but I wasn't sure why or what they intended to do with us. Sometimes people came along and then one of us would leave. I didn't know if that was good or bad but Ginger next door told me that if we weren't able to find homes soon they would take us to a big room where someone in a white coat would stick a needle in to make us sleep forever. I had no idea how I could find myself a home or what this needle was but sleeping *forever* didn't sound good - even if I did like to nap all day. I heard Jack telling someone that they never did this to cats unless they were very old or sick but it seemed to me that keeping us here in these basic little huts was neither going to make us younger or fitter, now was it?

I ate my breakfast in silence, ignoring the mad tabby on the other side of me. He always made a racket about everything and today he didn't like his food and was spitting it all over the floor. Louise came over and stroked him but he lashed his big fat paw out at her and she let out a loud shriek. If this was his way of getting a new home he was going about it the wrong way. I finished eating and pulled my blanket over my dish so no one could see I still had a little left. I'd have that later.

I had a funny feeling that today was going to be different but I didn't know why. Sometimes cats just *know* things. I hoped it was something good rather than something bad - but it was definitely *something*.

Human people started coming in and stared through the bars. I crawled into my little blue plastic box that I used as a bed and tried to make myself really small to hide myself from everyone. None of these humans seemed very polite or kind and they all *stared* so. I hated being looked at and I tried not to let anyone see me. I slipped into my inner pod when they were looking outside and when they come indoors I slipped into my outer cage so they couldn't see me either. It wasn't that I didn't want a new home - I did. I wanted one badly. It was just that I didn't want *any* old home. I needed somewhere quiet where I could be spoilt *rotten*. Being pampered is very important to me.

Today I must have got confused or nodded off at the wrong time because a pretty woman with yellowy-white hair and a high pitched voice came towards me before I could escape. She had an older lady with her and she was saying very loudly, 'Here she is Mum – Kimmy. Number thirteen. Unlucky for some'.

I cringed and tried to make my escape but it was too late. They had already seen me and I wondered if they'd brought food. They were reading my name and details that had been written on a large piece of paper with a photo. It was stuck to the side of my cage and I'd been told that I was ***Pet of the Week***. Well, that was hardly surprising. I thought I was pet of the year! But having this title meant that I was special even more so than usual. It looked as if these people had come straight to my cage and not bothered looking at any of the other cats.

The woman was reading from the notes by my door. 'It says she is ten years old ….'

'That's right! Tell everyone,' I fumed.

'And has been here since March,' said the other.

It's hardly good for a cat's confidence - *not* being chosen for a long time.

'That's just when I moved to Bath,' exclaimed the younger one reading on. 'Tabby, female,' she said.

'Tabby *and* white,' I said through gritted teeth. Don't forget my white bits!

I tried to make myself even smaller, hoping to become invisible until I heard one of them tell the other that I would be ideal for her big house. *Big.*

'I could spoil her rotten Mum,' she said.

The other woman agreed that this indeed would be very possible. My ears by now had completely pricked up. I don't speak fluent human but I know a good many words and I did know that what I wanted most and what she was offering was to spoil me. She also said she had a large house. This was starting to sound good and even Ginger from next door was listening in.

Jack had now joined the two women and was telling them that I was 'lovely' and 'very friendly'. Oh, well done Jack!

Ginger took a loud pee in his litter tray and a horrid smell drifted into my cage. He was trying to spoil my chances! Really I didn't think

I could stand this any more. I decided to look up at the women and make a little crying sound that humans always like.

'Mew,' …. I said as pathetically as I could and both women went all gooey and silly.

'Poor little thing. I think she likes you,' said the older one. It always amazed me how easy it was to impress humans. If I did a little mew like I do all the time, but in the right way, it was enough to make them putty in my paws.

'Can I hold her?' asked one and Jack, to my amazement, agreed. I hated it when strangers wanted to pick me up. But today I knew it was important and I allowed Jack to lift me up, place me in the other woman's arms and I relaxed. For a human, she smelt very nice. I began to purr and it was a long time since I'd done that.

The two women started to laugh and make stupid noises but I knew they liked me and I was surprised when they put me back and walked away.

'Hey, why are you going? Why aren't you taking me with you?' I screamed as they walked off.

Ginger started to sneeze and threw me a look, his nose dribbling moisture. He got back into his cat lit tray. He was disgusting.

Jack returned me to my cage and whispered to me, 'Well done Kimmy. I think you've found a new home'.

But by the end of the day I was still here and the disappointment was more than I could bear. I went to sleep cold and miserable. So much for today being special.

Top Tip

If you have the misfortune to find yourself at a Cats' Home

looking for a new family do NOT be sitting on the litter tray or stuffing your face when humans are walking past. Even worse DON'T be scrapping with the cat next door.

DO look as appealing as possible. Keep yourself exceptionally well groomed. Sit up straight with your head inclined to one side looking sad or - even better (for exceptional circumstances) - roll on your back letting everyone see your tummy. You'll have a new home in no time!

Thursday 17th May

As if yesterday wasn't bad enough, today was even worse. It seemed that Ginger had someone interested in him. Like many of the cats resident at this Home Ginger had the appearance of a cat who had been in one fight too many. His face, possibly pretty as a kitten, was now scarred and lopsided. But now a badly dressed woman chewing something that made her mouth go round and round and side to side came to talk to him. I heard Jack say that he was 'available'. I used all my powers to hide myself still further. Ginger would never let me forget that he got a home before I did. He'd only been here for a few weeks! I tried not to watch as the woman stroked the red monster through his cage.

'Wait till you smell his cat litter tray first thing,' I tried to tell her but Ginger was rolling over and playing all stupid like I'd never seen him do before. He must be desperate to get out of here!

And then – a miracle. The ladies from yesterday came back and this time there were two other people with them.

'Kimmy!' said the younger one excitedly from behind the glass door that kept me from the rest of the world. Of course I couldn't hear her, just see her lips moving and I don't always understand every single thing that humans say anyway, although I knew my name.

Jack opened the door and they crowded in to my small cell. I can see that there is a new sign on my door saying **'First Reserve'**. Someone did want to take me home! I'd seen that sign before on the side of a cage and then a few days later the cat would leave.

'Kimmy' said the kind lady now kneeling beside where I was sitting on my blanket. She began to stroke me. This time, thankfully, she had brought food. I ate the snack sticks she pulled out of the packet while she told me that this was her mother, sister and her sister's friend. Blimey, was I going to be living with all of them? That sounded very crowded. I munched on the chicken bits and tried not to watch Ginger with his big fat legs in the air having his stomach stroked. It nearly put me off my food.

The woman rubbed my back and told me that her name was Christine and that she was going to be my 'New Mum'.

'Just as soon as I get my home visit done,' she told me. Yes please, do get your home checked for me. *Check it thoroughly.* Make sure it has no dogs, no small children, lots of beds and cushions for me to sit on - oh, and a nice garden too if possible. She placed a soft toy in my plastic bed. Did she think I'm a kitten? I am a fully-grown, mature cat. But I purred my appreciation because I was not stupid. Then I lifted my hind leg and began to lick myself energetically. It was good to show them that I had fastidious cleanliness. I could see them admiring my long furry limbs.

Her whole family were now making loud cooing noises as they stared in at me. I had four admirers after having had none for so long.

It felt good to be adored again and I made the most of it. I glanced next door to see that sly Ginger was watching.

To my delight I saw three disgustingly dirty and noisy kids appearing from nowhere and crowding around Ginger's cage. One was chewing gum and another was carrying an ice cream that was dripping. Some of it fell and landed on his fur. I hated that happening to me. I always like to be immaculate. Ginger's new home was obviously to be with this woman and her children. They will pull his tail and wake him every time he tried to sleep. Suddenly I was not jealous any more. My arch-enemy was going to some low-rent, high rise flat somewhere where he'd be lucky to get more than own-brand cat food and exercise on a balcony. I shuddered at the thought. Whereas I, from the look of it, was going to a woman who seemed potty about me. And she was someone who had promised to 'spoil me rotten' in her great big house. I would hold her to that!

'Goodbye Kimmy,' she said just as I was getting used to her strange smell. Not bad but just different.

'No! You can't go! You have to take me with you ....!'

The woman looked back sadly.

'We'll be back soon Kimmy!' she said. 'And hopefully next time I'll be taking you with me!'

I'd got a new home! Hadn't I?

Friday 18th May

Soon after yet another breakfast I saw Jack stuffing Ginger's huge body into what seemed like a tiny little box and carrying him off. I hoped he was not to be put to sleep! Even though I hated him I would never wish that on anyone. But the lovely Jack saw my look of fear as he struggled to secure the catches on his travelling case.

'Say goodbye to Ginger, Kimmy. He's off to a lovely … er a new home – and it'll be your turn next'. His legs had almost buckled from the weight of carrying him.

I really hoped so. I heard Ginger fart as he went past and I dived into my outside pod.I couldn't believe he'd found a home before me. What were people thinking?

But then the Christine person came to see me again and once again, she'd brought me food. This time I couldn't help but show a little less interest in her because if Ginger could leave why couldn't I? She told me that she still hadn't had one of those home visit thingies and couldn't take me home until then. I stared at her unblinkingly. I thought she was making excuses. I kept my options open by nuzzling her hand - just in case

I heard her talking to Louise and being told that the home visitors were all volunteers so she would have to be patient. I had no idea what a 'volunteer' was but Christine got cross and said something about, 'I'm sick of waiting. I could do better myself'. And then she left again.

(Note from Kimmy's Mum; Kimmy is being a bit unfair here about Ginger. A home in a flat is perfectly acceptable provided the cat is either older or has never been used to a garden. If a cat suffers from the very common FIV disease, then they will have to live in a flat so they don't mix with other cats. It is not necessary to be rich or live in a big house to be a good cat owner.)

Saturday 19th May

I was still here! Another day waking up in this noisy cell, the sound of banging doors all around me. So much for the new home that I had been promised.

There was a new cat next to me where Ginger used to be. She appeared to be a very timid Persian, or Iranian as they really are now – very posh. I knew that I *should* say nice things to her to let her know that life here isn't too bad and that she'd probably get a home soon but I really couldn't be bothered. I was still so disappointed that the new home I had been promised hadn't happened. Christine hadn't even come to see me today and that could only mean that she had changed her mind or that her house wasn't good enough. I ignored the pathetic cries from 'Princess' next door and tried to concentrate on having a good nap. Saturdays were very busy here and there were so many people. I didn't want them to see me so I had to keep moving either inside or out so that they never found me. But wouldn't you know it? Princess had been here just five minutes and a nice looking lady had asked to reserve her. This was so unfair! What had she got that I hadn't?

Finally the Home closed and Jack said goodbye to us all and went off to his home. I was left all alone in my cage with just the howls of the dogs across the way to keep me awake. It is awful here at night-time. That's when all the animals get very lonely and start to cry. Some miss their old friends, others find it hard to settle here but we all want a new family to take us home. I was really sad and wished Christine had come to see me. I shouted at Princess to, 'be quiet,' because she was wailing in much the way I was feeling and Peter the tabby next door had a big scratch (I hoped he hadn't given me fleas). I was cold and fed up and finally I went to sleep. Zzzzzzzzzzzzzzzzz.

Sunday 20th May

Would you believe it but Christine turned up this morning! She told me she had been waiting by the phone all of yesterday for the home visitors to ring her.

'They didn't ring Kimmy,' she told me as she climbed into my cage and sat down with me. I was so pleased to see her that I let her pick me up and put me on her knee. I relaxed and began to purr. People stopped as they walked by and started to laugh - but not at me, they were laughing at Christine! They thought it was funny to find a human sitting in a cat's cage. A few of them asked if she was up for adoption but I thought it was brilliant of her to come into my home like this and I licked her hand to show my appreciation. For some reason her eyes filled with tears.

'Oh Kimmy, I can't wait to get you home'.

I couldn't wait either.

(Note from Kimmy's Mum; to be fair to Bath Cats and Dogs Home, home visits don't normally take this long. You can usually expect to wait between 1 – 3 days but the checkers are volunteers and have other lives. Sometimes, as in this case, they go away on holiday).

Monday 21st May

As if life wasn't bad enough. The posh lady from just yesterday came to pick up Princess who gave me a smug look at she glided into a travelling box with a fur blanket in the bottom. How come her new person got a home visit before mine? Even Louise thought it was unfair although she didn't actually say that.

'It'll be you next Kimmy,' she said as she scooped food onto a plate for my breakfast but I felt very depressed today. I decided to stay in the east wing

The Home was quiet, as the outside people weren't allowed in today so I wouldn't be able to see Christine. A small black cat was put in the cage next to me where Ginger and Princess used to be. He was tiny but quite feisty and started to make hissing noises at me through the wire.

'Purr-lease! You've been here five minutes. Don't build your part!' Eventually he stopped and went away.

Louise came to tell me that Christine was having her home check that evening.

'You might be going to a new home tomorrow,' she said. I huddled in my box. I'd been disappointed before so I wouldn't get my hopes up. With my luck 'Mr Hissy' next to me would be out before me. I tried to settle down to go to sleep but I was cold and hungry. Could this be my last night here after all?

Tuesday 22nd May

Christine turned up just as the Home opened and she seemed very excited. I heard her talking to Louise outside my cage.

'I've passed Louise. Jan came round and we spoke for ages and I've just heard that it's okay for me to take Kimmy home, just as soon as she's been to the vet. When do you think that might be? Is the vet here?'

I knew Jan. She was the lady who took our pictures to put up on the sides of our cages and for the in-ter-net. She had agreed to do the visit because the person who should have done had gone away. She's dead nice and smiles a lot. She always managed to make us look our best even when we were quite ugly. She told me that she got her cat Mickey from here but she didn't offer to take *me* home. Still, if she'd passed Christine she must be okay but what was that about the vet?

Louise opened my cage door and Christine bounced in. Her face was all lit up and she was talking very fast. I pulled away.

'Kimmy darling, you're going to the vet …'

'Oh no! Not the dreaded needle!' I cringed back into my cage and tried to make myself go all heavy. My fur stood up in spikes.

'And then I am going to be able to take you home!'

Louise smiled in at me, 'Kimmy just let me pop you in your box and you'll be home in no time'.

'Home? What is that? I used to have a home and now *this* is my home. Suddenly somewhere else is going to be my home'. I felt very scared. Louise picked me up gently and Christine held the lid of a carrying box while I was put inside struggling as much as I could. Christine gathered up my things - my blue plastic box and the toys she brought me but I notice she had left my food behind!

I was now so scared that I thought I might wet my box. What was going on? I'd seen this happen to other cats and knew that somehow it was good but right now all I could feel was fear. What was happening to me? Had I become a real scaredy-cat? I was carried along in my box and I saw everything as I passed it - the dogs in the pen across the way whose barking used to wake me up and the guinea pigs and rabbits over the other side who I had not seen before. Louise walked too fast and I couldn't take anything in. I felt uncomfortable and nervous in the small cramped space and desperately wanted to get out. My mouth felt dry and I wanted to cry but not much came out when I opened my mouth.

And then I was put on a table where the lady in the white coat looked at me and smiled. I looked to see if she was holding a needle. She wasn't.

'Hello nice cat,' she said. 'Just let me take a look and then you'll be okay to go to your new home'.

She pulled and prodded at me for a few moments and I didn't close my eyes. I didn't want to let her sneak out that needle! Louise kept telling me that I was okay and a 'good girl' but what choice did I have? If it were up to me I'd be legging it right now as far away as I could get. Was this where all those other cats ended up – like Ginger and Princess? Did their lives end here with this lady?

But I was handed back to Louise and bundled back into my box and taken out to where Christine was waiting for me. She was sitting at a table in the big, busy crowded area where people first come into when they visit the Home. She was signing some papers and talking very fast and excitedly and she ignored me. I now felt even worse than I did a moment ago - if that was possible. But then she finished what she was doing at the table. She folded some pieces of paper and put them with her handbag and turned to me and said, 'Kimmy sweetheart, now I am taking you to your new home'.

New home? So I was really having a new home? But what if she didn't like me or feed me the right food? Did she know what I liked? I began to panic again and opened my mouth to cry, 'Help!' but nothing much came out. Christine was talking to someone on something small she pulled from her handbag to ask for what she calls 'a taxi'. I had no idea what this was and felt even more scared. She turned to Louise and thanked her by doing that silly thing humans do - she shook her hand and then she suddenly hugged her. Louise looked as crushed as I had been a few moments ago. Right now, I just wanted to get out of this tiny box and run and run and run as far away as I could go. The last time I was in this box was when my old family took me to the Home and left me. I can honestly say that every time I went in this carrier something not very good happened to me. This place may not have been the warmest, most comfortable place in the world and I never, ever got enough food or attention but the people were very kind to me. Would Louise and Jack be coming too? Would they come to see me? Oh, why had no one explained all this to me?

Top Tip

If you are lucky enough to get adopted from Bath Cats and

Dogs Home make sure your 'New Mum' leaves a good donation when she takes you home. It helps all the animals that are still in the Home looking for families. If she can't afford it, is she really the right Mum for you?

Chapter Two

New Home

The car pulled up outside the doors to the Home. I hadn't seen these for months - since I arrived to be precise and I'd hardly noticed them then. I was carried to the back and put on a padded seat where I couldn't see anything or look out at where I was going. I tried to relax but it was impossible and I breathed very, very slowly to calm myself. I remembered the food I'd left in my bowl and wondered if anyone else would eat it now I'd left the Home or whether this person, Christine, had brought it with her after all.

After being jiggled about *forever* we stopped the car on what seemed like a very noisy road with lots and lots of cars. Christine gave the man some money and took me in my box from the back seat. She carried me very slowly and carefully and I was grateful for that because I had no idea where I was or how I would get back from there to anywhere if I was dropped. I heard a lot of wheels - and the sound scared me. I could feel all my fur tense up and stand in firm clumps at the back of my neck. Some of the cats at the Home had stitches and bandages on places that had been hit by these things and many of them told me that they were 'lucky' as they could have been killed. I am not sure how only having three legs instead of four or having broken bones could be called 'lucky', but they always said that. Now there I was being carried with all these dangerous cars whizzing past me. I closed my eyes and really hoped that I would be okay.

Christine fumbled in her bag for a moment - but it felt like ages - to find something that she used to open the door. I was so relieved that once again I nearly wet myself. In an instant we were inside and safe. She closed the door behind us and then she closed another door inside the room. It seemed to make the noise go away and it was much quieter then.

'Now Kimmy,' said Christine, opening the front of my carrier so that I could get out, 'this is your new home now. And I am your 'New Mum'. I'm your Mum.'

'New Mum' or no 'New Mum' I felt the most horrible, dreadful fear that I had ever felt in my life. I had no idea where I was or who this person was but suddenly my life had changed all over again and this time I didn't have Louise, Jack or even Jan around to protect me. Even seeing Ginger's ugly face right now would have made me feel a lot better.

I am ashamed to say that I was so scared that I didn't even look around me. I just ran. I tried to run as far away as I could from this woman who called herself 'New Mum' and I went down a deep wooden staircase then along and into a room with a tall window where I could only see people's ankles as they walked past on the street above, where I had come in. It had a thick soft, woolly floor and a bed that I ran under. It was cool and dark. This was the most space I had seen for a long time and I suddenly felt very tiny. My heart was pounding inside my body.

'New Mum' sighed and a few minutes later she brought down a

litter tray and, much to my surprise, my little blue plastic box from my old cage at the Home. She put the litter just outside, in the room next to where I was but I could see it. She went off again and then joy of joys she brought back some food. A big plate of what looked like Whiskas was placed on a mat on the floor. It certainly smelt like Whiskas. How did she know this was my favourite? I felt a little more cheerful. 'New Mum' then put a blue blanket down beside the dish. 'In case you want to pull it over your food afterwards,' she said. But that made no sense. There were no other cats here why would I want to hide my food? But I supposed she was trying to be kind. It was just that I felt so unsure of myself. I stayed down in this room until it got dark outside. 'New Mum' came down a lot to see me but I hid and she had to look for me by checking all the cupboards and then kneeling on the floor and looking under the bed.

When I was feeling a little braver and I thought that 'New Mum' has gone to bed, I sneaked a look around the room next to me – it had big wooden curtains that covered the glass doors and my litter tray was there – that's not quite as private as I would have liked it. No cat really wants people to see her 'going', like they did at the Home. The floor was cold and hard under my paws and felt totally different to the softness of the other room with the bed. It smelt different too. Sort of *colder*. There was a bathroom with one of those shower things that humans like to use and a cupboard where I could hide if I needed to. 'New Mum' had closed the curtains in my room now so I couldn't see the feet as they walked past - but I could hear strange noises - like the washing machine which seemed to bounce across the floor above me. I wasn't used to this but then everything here was new to me. I did sort of remember what this sound was from my old home but my life had changed so much recently. I thought I wanted a new home but now I just wanted to go back to the Cats and Dogs Home and my safe little cage with the people and cats that I knew. Sorry but this isn't going to be easy, I thought as I settled down under the bed. I was too scared to close my eyes.

I had a 'New Mum' and a new house. This was all far, far too strange for one day. I tucked my paws under me and I slowly drifted off into a light doze otherwise known as a cat nap.

Wednesday 23rd May

I couldn't think where I was when I first woke. There was light coming through a gap in the curtain and I could hear lots of noises – different noises from the Home - footsteps walking past very fast as if lots of people were in a hurry to get somewhere. I was under the bed with a warm carpet beneath me and smells I just didn't recognise. There were no other cats around and no dogs howling and hurling themselves against the front of their cages. I licked my lips nervously. Then I heard footsteps on the stairs so I ran again - this time into the bathroom and a cupboard that I had found before. I hurried inside and tried to hold my breath and make myself invisible. But the door opened and she was standing there – Christine - 'New Mum'. She was wearing a funny long coat-thing over her sleep clothes, tied at the waist and her hair was all untidy. Her eyes had gone all baggy since I'd last seen her and she was rubbing them. 'Morning Kimmy,' she said and held up a dish of food for me.

Oh, that's nice! I was very hungry and it was my favourite, chicken Whiskas! I nervously sidled out and cowered towards the food. 'New

Mum' stroked my head and I let her. Then she went off and a little later came back down dressed differently. She'd smoothed her eyes out too. I'd gone back under the bed.

'Kimmy!' she called and she opened the shutters to reveal, to my surprise, that there was a small garden outside with a nice safe wall around it. There was no grass just stone paving and a great big tree at the back growing up the brickwork. That's exactly what I always dreamed of (the safe wall, that is - I would have liked grass). But it was secure and somewhere I could prowl without running into any danger.

Later 'New Mum' tried to get me to come up the stairs. 'Come on Kimmy,' she said gently. I was fairly sure that she was kind and I would have liked to go up and see what was up there but I was just too anxious. A few moments later she then came down with a small table and put one of those things that humans tap their fingers across to make words on a screen. She told me that she was a writer and that this was her laptop. Not a television, although it has pictures on it too. She plugged it in and started to make click, click, clicking noises, her face all scrunched up as she worked. Occasionally she would make snorting noises as if amused by what she was doing. Sometimes her tongue would come out, like mine does. Every now and again she smiled at me.

'If I can't get you to come up to me, I'll come down to you!' she said as she carried on making those little tapping sounds with her fingers. I thought that it was probably okay to go up but I was just not sure enough yet. I looked at the wooden stairs and wondered if I would be brave enough. It would help if I knew where they led to but I felt safe where I was. Up there looked scary. 'New Mum' brought me food and I had water and a cat lit tray and now I could see out into the garden and I could watch the lady working at her desk near me. That's okay for now. That's all quite enough.

'New Mum' went off and changed again - this time into funny shorts and a top that was also slightly short. She had socks and springy big white shoes on and she was jumping around from foot to foot doing what she called 'warming up'. Did she know how silly she looked?

'I'm going to my running club Kimmy,' she said and for a minute I wanted to start crying again. I didn't want her to go out. I needed her full attention but she was heading off now and I heard the door slam and saw her funny rubbery shoes pass the window of my bedroom. She'd left me on my own! How could she spoil me if she wasn't even here? But that is exactly what she'd done. I settled down for a nap to take my mind off things.

Later she returned with a hot, red looking face and took a long shower in the bathroom that I thought of as mine and came out all wet and shiny. She didn't really look much different though so I wondered what good she thought that running very fast had done her. She played with me for a while by lying on the floor and tickling me and I wanted her to stay with me for longer. She told me she had to go and dry off and get changed.

What sort of an excuse was that? I was sorry to say that I hit her with my paw - my claws making contact with her damp skin and she gave a little cry.

'Kimmy!'

Okay. So we don't always like ourselves.

Top tip

If you find yourself in a new home, take a few days to settle in without any fuss. Find a quiet room that you can make your own. Hopefully your Mum will let you have the peace to do that.

Thursday 24th May

'New Mum' brought food down to me the next day and I was impressed. She seemed to have got it just right. A nice big plate of what tasted like chicken Whiskas again in jelly. I ate it slowly as I was being watched and I wanted her to note that I liked it. Then maybe she would give it to me again.

She pulled back the big white wooden shutters and lots of sunlight streamed in. I blinked. Then much to my surprise she opened the glass doors and I started to walk towards them. Maybe this was an escape route? I was not sure why I would want to run away as I didn't yet feel brave enough to go up the stairs. I didn't really want to do a runner - but a cat likes to have options.

'New Mum' said, 'No,' to me. She spoke really sharply and loudly. She'd never spoken like that to me before.

'No Kimmy - not outside today. You're not allowed out for at least … er, a month'.

A month! Was she mad? That little garden with the wall was about the size of the outside runs that some of the big dogs had at the Home. Did she really think she could keep me from it? What did she really think that I would do? But I settled for watching as she gathered up lots of pots and began to shake some brown stuff from a bag in them. It looked a little like the cat litter in my tray and would make a good place for me to use instead of the loo inside. I made a note and marvelled at how busy humans can look when they're doing very little.

She came back in and went up the stairs and for a moment I felt like following her but something just stopped me and instead I ran and hid under the bed - again.

I don't know why but my heart was beating like the feathers of one of the birds I see flying past me in the sky. Like when they're trapped but know you're looking at them. I felt really shy again. I decided I wouldn't be coming out from under there until I didn't feel like this any more.

Friday 25th May

'New Mum' did the same thing again today. She opened the big wooden shutters and started to open the door. Sunlight began to pour into the hall like milk spilt from a bottle. I latched myself onto her ankle and began to purr.

'You want to come out Kim?' she asked. I ignored her as I don't like being called Kim.

'Kimmy?' she repeated. I purred my reply. 'Well just for a moment then'.

We went out into the funny little garden with the table and chairs (why do people put furniture outside when it's always raining?) and this time she had a little can with a spout and put water on the little pots that she filled with the brown stuff yesterday. I closed my eyes for a second and breathed in the new smell. It was all clean and fresh, a little chill and the faint smell of leaves and flowers in pots. She watched me very closely but there was no need. I was just enjoying the feeling that I was not shut in anywhere - the first time I had felt like this for a long time. No one was keeping me where I didn't want to be. She hadn't locked me in or stopped me from going out. I had wanted to do something and I'd been allowed to. The feel of the sunlight on my fur was fantastic. I felt warm and comfortable and safer than I'd felt for a long, long time. I rolled over for a moment allowing myself to stretch in the dust not minding the gritty feel of it in my fur. Then I got back on my paws again. I could hear a bird somewhere and I looked up to see where it was. 'New Mum' caught me looking up at the sky.

'Oh no you don't Kimmy! No looking for ways to escape over the wall'. She scooped her hand under me and shooed me back inside. Then she shut the doors behind me. I was impressed that she thought I could scale a wall that high. But I certainly didn't want to even if I could. I had had a moment of freedom and it felt wonderful. Next time I had better not look upwards …!

Then she tried to coax me up the stairs. This time, perhaps encouraged by my little trip outside, I really wanted to go and I began to climb - first one stair, (it felt strange, not soft like the room with the bed but hard and slippery) then another and I got about halfway when I just felt my heart again. Boom, boom … then I froze and ran back downstairs and hid under the bed again. I didn't really know stairs as I didn't have them at my last home. It felt odd to be climbing like this. They felt slippery under my body. But I was beginning to know I was safe here and even though I knew 'New Mum' was upstairs and that she was kind, I was too nervous to go up there. I waited a while but I heard her moving about above me and eventually I just got too curious and began to climb again …

This time, I didn't run back and at the top I saw a room with a wooden floor, like the stairs, and a big, very comfortable looking sofa in the sort of material that I like to sit on. I didn't know the colour as we cats don't bother ourselves with details like that unless we have to. But it was different to the floor. Brighter. On the other side was a kitchen. 'New Mum' was really pleased to see me and made a big fuss. She gave me food (always the way to a cat's heart) and stroked me for ages. Then she went off and got one of those things that humans use to get pictures of us, like Jan at the Home. I like having my picture done and I posed like mad. All cats like to be admired and being the focus of attention. Later that night I fell asleep on the sofa and it was as comfortable as it looked. Oh, this was wonderful. I thought I was going to like it here.

Top Tip

If your Mum keeps calling you by a name that you don't like - just ignore her and pretend you haven't heard. Eventually she will get the message and call you by a name you prefer.

Saturday 26th May

At some point of the night I must have woken up and wondered where I was because in the morning I was back huddled under the bed again when 'New Mum' came down. She had to look for me.

'Oh Kimmy!' she said when she found me (surprisingly quickly). 'I wish you wouldn't feel you had to hide from me! I thought you liked it upstairs?'

She fed me and talked to me and then we went out into the courtyard again. This time she was drinking a cup of coffee, sitting at the table and I decided to sun myself a bit. I rolled around on the ground and looked up at the sky. I'd missed seeing the sun without wire netting in my way. I could feel its gentle heat on my exposed, full-of-food tummy.

She went inside and hesitantly I followed. I liked to be where she was because she made me feel safe. This time I decided I would go upstairs again. Downstairs had got boring and if 'New Mum' spent so much time up there maybe it was interesting?

I climbed up the stairs slowly, taking one step at a time until there were no more and I was in the big room again. 'New Mum' was lying on the sofa where I was planning to sleep like I had last night and she was reading some big bits of paper. She had beaten me to the sofa!

'Oh Kimmy! How lovely to see you.'

I ran to meet the hand she stretched out. She began to stroke me and I felt really warm and comfortable. This really was the way I liked to be treated. I felt her fingers gently caressing my back and I purred like a big fat train - not that I am fat of course, just well covered.

I took a little jump so I landed right on her tummy. She made a funny sort of yelping noise as I landed on top of her. It was soft and comfortable and I began to purr again. A moment later I was asleep and we stayed like that until 'New Mum' finished what she was doing and had to get up. She gently pushed me off.

'New Mum' then suggested I follow her up to what she called the drawing-room. I didn't know what that was. Was it somewhere to do drawing? Shouldn't it be writing if that was what she did? Or maybe the downstairs hall was the 'writing room'? There was another flight of stairs to go up and I was unsure. These steps were lovely and soft and warm under my paws and I felt myself sink into them. This would be good to manicure my rather long nails on, I thought. I took one step and then another and I went higher up the stairs each time. A moment later I was in another strange room but this one was even better than the last! It was a big room with the soft floor and had furniture that was all made from stuff I liked to sit on. It was warm and more comfortable than anything you could ever imagine. I thought of Ginger and wanted to purr even louder. He was probably at his new home at the top of a big building squashed on a sofa with his whole smelly family. It couldn't be anything as nice as this. 'New Mum' put on that noisy box with the pictures of funny people. The sound scared me and I turned to run back down.

'Kimmy!' she made the noise go away by pointing something at it. It went quiet and she put her hand out to me. I made myself stay and I settled down on the soft floor to have a little nap after all that exertion. I supposed it would be asking a bit much for her to bring me a snack but a cat can dream.

I slept and dozed and stretched out my paw just to make sure that my new world was still here. It was and I felt happy.

Sunday 27th May

I woke up feeling really scared. The room where I had been sleeping was no longer warm and comfortable and 'New Mum' wasn't there. In fact, I wasn't even quite sure where I was. The noisy box stared silently back at me, cold and empty of pictures. I felt very alone. It was also very dark and I was not sure which way to go to get back to the comfort of the other room where I could hide under the bed. Should I go up? Or down? I tried to remember where I should be and where she might be and I asked myself where I was right now and it all felt too much for me. I started to cry and cry and couldn't stop. The sound of my crying got louder. In the silence of the night it sounded very loud indeed.

I didn't hear the footsteps on the stairs but I felt the warm arms around me as I was picked up from where I was lying. All of a sudden I felt the comfort of something beating against my face. 'New Mum's' heart. Something inside the person that felt comfortable and soothing. I felt her soft, wobbly bits at the front of her body and I cried with gratitude at her finding me when I was feeling so miserable. *Mew* …

She carried me very gently up the stairs I'd not climbed before. More stairs. Oh, was there more to this house? It really was huge. At the top she carried me into a room I hadn't been in before and placed me on a big warm bed, much bigger than the one downstairs and she got in herself. I was going to be allowed to sleep with 'New Mum' in this lovely quiet room in a cosy bed! I thought of Ginger again lying on his nylon bedspread that he'd probably have to share with a stinky dog and I shuddered. I snuggled up next to her and begin to purr just as loud as I could. I felt 'New Mum's' hand on my back and suddenly she wasn't 'New Mum' – she was just 'Mum'. My Mum. And this was my lovely new place to live. At last I was home.

Chapter Three

Settling In

Later on when Mum had gone out I decided that it was time I checked out the whole of my new house to see if it was suitable accommodation for a cat who wanted to be as spoilt as I do. Mum had already told me that it is over two hundred years old. I wonder how many cats have lived here before me. Does anyone know anything about cats from the old days?

The very top of the house has the big bedroom with the bed that is now mine, but I share it with Mum. It has a soft floor, a big window and those wooden doors that open and close to block the light and the darkness out. And it had lots of interesting looking cupboards with mirrors on where I could admire myself. I liked the cupboards, as they were great places to hide when life got a bit scary.

Next to the bedroom is a bathroom with a big high bath on funny feet and there is another window with a seat where I could sit and look out if I wanted. But it is so high up I would be scared looking down all that way. There was nowhere cosy for me to lie in this room so I don't suppose I will use it much.

Down one flight of stairs was the big drawing room, as Mum calls it. It had a huge window each end and in another corner there is another small window. They all have those wooden curtainey things like the doors downstairs and the bedroom upstairs. The furniture was dead posh and Mum told me that nearly everything was new as she had just moved here from a small flat in London. I like that, no rubbish for Kimmy!

I padded down the stairs to see what was below. It was the big room with the sofa and table made of something see through like the window where I could see people walking by. That's funny, in my last home the tables were made of wood. Next to it was the kitchen. I noticed that Mum had now moved my little dishes upstairs and they were now in a row along the floor. She had put all my food in a cupboard that she called 'Kimmy's cupboard' and I hoped it would always be kept full. There was another window at the back with a seat from where I could see the garden below.

Down the stairs from there (and does this house go on forever?) is the room where I spent my first few days - the bedroom with a window that shows people's feet as they walk past. There is a room with a shower next door. Outside is another room with a big cupboard under the stairs and my not-so-private loo. There were the double glass doors that sometimes have the shutters over them and when they were open I could go out to the funny little garden with the wall and no grass, but lots of pots. It had a huge tree that takes up most of it, its green branches acting almost like a roof on the small courtyard. I had this whole place to myself - well, I have to share it with Mum - and the little birds that fly in and out.

Now I had seen the house I could settle down for a nap and wait until I was thoroughly spoiled again.

Tuesday 29th May

I watched as Mum laid out a mat on the floor - it was like the mat I ate my food off only bigger. Then she went to the box and turned on some funny pictures. The next thing I saw was her kneeling on all fours - like a cat - doing the sort of exercises I do all the time. She was doing big stretches with her hands in front of her on the floor. After that she had one leg right up in the air. That couldn't be natural? Next she was standing on one leg. Surely not? And then finally, just when I was getting quite stressed watching her, she lay on her back with her arms outstretched by her side and her eyes closed.

I panicked. Was she unwell? Who would feed me if she didn't wake up? So I jumped on top of her tummy and dug in my claws. She screamed.

It turned out she was doing something called 'yoga' and lying on the floor pretending to be asleep was part of it.

Humans can be very funny.

Friday 1st June

Although I have a pretty sunny personality I woke up feeling a bit moody. Maybe it was the weather because it had suddenly got quite chilly again. Mum didn't open the doors to the garden today. We cats don't like it when it is cold. Mum seemed in a bit of bad mood too so I decided to keep to myself in the room downstairs where the bed is cosy. It was not as big as my bed upstairs but during the day, I don't have to share it with Mum. I could see a bit of people's legs as they walked past but they could see all of me on the bed and sometimes they stopped to admire me - especially the children who were closer to the window and saw me better. I liked this a lot as I love it when people appreciate and admire me even though their shrieks and cries woke me up.

Mum thought I was unhappy and kept bringing me down different food to try. Usually I would love this attention but today I just wanted to be left alone. I've come a long way in a short time and I needed to think it all through.

Top Tip

Never be afraid to pull the odd 'sickie'. This doesn't have to be too serious (or you'll be packed off to the vet's) but every now and again just be a little 'off colour'. This should result in extra food and lots of extra attention.

Saturday 2nd June

The sun shone again and I woke up in a good mood. Mum put on shorts and sat out in the little garden. I came out to join her. She'd put a little bed out there for me and I climbed in and settled down for a snooze. I loved sleeping in the sunshine as it warmed my fur and made me feel better. Mum brought my food down to eat and told me that we were dining al fresco (whatever that was). I slept like this all day. Bliss ....

Tuesday 5th June

Something very odd happened today. I heard Mum on the phone to someone asking if they were a 'Cat Feeder'. Why would Mum want a cat feeder when she did that herself? Did she plan to get someone else to get my meals for me? That was *very* posh.

A lady came round much later. She had driven in a little van which she parked outside although Mum warned her that there was a double yellow line there (whatever that was. Maybe the paint was still wet? I knew about wet paint). She sat with Mum at the table and I listened from halfway up the stairs. I couldn't hear all of it but after they had said a great deal and the new lady had written things down on a piece of paper, I heard Mum say, 'Would you like to meet Kimmy? See how you get on.' I turned and ran for it because I didn't like the look of this new 'cat feeder' and I thought Mum was very lazy not doing that herself. I ran downstairs and hid under the bed. A few moments later I saw two faces peering at me upside down.

'Hello Kimmy,' said the new lady. Her face looked all funny from this angle.

Mum was frowning. 'I'm sorry, I don't know why she is so timid but I'm sure she'll be okay for you'.

What does that mean, 'Okay for you'? Was I being passed on to a new home again? I thought about it for a little while. And then I threw up on the carpet.

(Note from Kimmy's Mum; this is a registered cat feeder and she is very good at her job. She will come to your home and feed your cat while you are away if you don't want to use a cattery or ask a friend. She is also a cat lover and loved Kimmy so she was being very mean hiding from her.)

Wednesday 6th June

I hadn't seen anything more of the 'cat feeder' but it was a lovely day again and I could see the sun in the sky. Mum and I sat out in the courtyard. It was funny but for someone who claimed to be a writer, she doesn't do much work really. When it's wet I heard her tapping away on her keyboard but days like today when it's hot - she just didn't bother. She sat around drinking coffee and reading magazines about 'celebrities'. Sometimes she chatted on the phone. Mum told me that most of what writers do goes on in 'their heads' but I thought that was just an excuse. I'd seen the books that lined the walls of her drawing room and knew that there had to be more to make that happen than just thinking. But when she did sit at her little desk she seemed much happier afterwards. If doing something made her happy it was hard to work out why she didn't do it more often but then I am only a cat.

Later she went out and left me alone so when she came back I sulked for a while. I'd lost all that time in the garden with sunshine on my fur and the cat feeder hadn't even been in to feed me.

Sunday 10th June

Every night I sleep on the big bed that I share with Mum. But I have noticed that she doesn't cat nap like I do. She goes into a deep sleep and she seems to sleep far too long. I woke up hungry and padded down the stairs to the kitchen. My bowl was empty! So much for the 'cat feeder'. I climbed back up the stairs and tried to attract Mum's attention. She was still asleep and wasn't listening to me and I couldn't make her open her eyes no matter how much I stared at her and prowled around the bed. She was like this after she'd done her yoga only then I could jump on her and wake her up. I started to pat her face and lick her hand. At the same time I purred as loudly as I could. That did the trick and Mum's eyes flickered open. 'Kimmy …oh how sweet, you're purring.' Humans love it when we purr. 'What time is it?' she shrieked. 'It is 4 am Kimmy!'

What was wrong with that? When a cat is hungry, she's hungry.

Mum groaned but got out of bed, slipped her feet into those funny knitted things she wore on them and began to walk slowly down the stairs. I ran on ahead, stopping to look behind me to make sure she was still with me. When I saw that she was I ran a bit further down the stairs. 'Keep up Mum!'

For some reason she found it funny watching me running down our stairs. They are very steep and a bit windy.

'I can see your bottom Kimmy. You're like a little bunny rabbit'.

Oh, whatever.

When we got to the kitchen, she put on a light and I patted the door of my cupboard just in case she didn't know what I was after. She yawned and began to pull out a packet of Whiskas and spooned it onto a plate.

'Oh Kimmy, I'm sorry,' she muttered. 'I mustn't be feeding you enough'.

I began to get busy with the food in front of me. I was starving! I thought how good this was. I got an early breakfast and I also managed to make Mum feel guilty. I was clearly getting the hang of this spoiling business!

Mum went back to bed. She was snoring when I went back up and leapt back on top of her.

Chapter Four

Elaine

Saturday 16th June

Mum's friend Elaine from London came to stay. She arrived last night and they sat about drinking and making a lot of noise. Elaine was very well dressed and pretty but I don't like strangers no matter what they look like. Mum hadn't lived in Bath long and didn't know many people but the few friends she had, came by and they drank a lot of that red stuff that makes humans talk even louder and behave so badly. I hid in the cupboard because I don't like strangers and I liked to be the centre of attraction, naturally. Most pampered cats will tell you that if their carers don't give them their full attention they start to feel very left out.

Today Mum and Elaine were going off on what they called shopping. I had breakfast on my usual little plate and scowled at Elaine who was trying to be nice to me.

I might have liked her better if she hadn't mentioned that she had a cat called Grace who was also a gorgeous tabby. Well, I hated it when other cats are mentioned so I kept my distance.

(Note from Kimmy's Mum; Elaine is a lovely person and she adores cats – especially her own cat Grace. She made a real effort

with Kimmy and was very, very kind to her. Kimmy behaved appallingly that weekend!)

Mum and Elaine had been out shopping for *ages*. I was bored and hungry when I heard Mum's key in the door and they fell into the room carrying so many bags of stuff that they were barely able to stand upright. They had had lunch at Bath's Pump Room. Whatever that was - expensive probably. Mum announced that, 'We can just take a break and then go back and do a bit more'.

More? Were they mad?

Elaine went down the stairs saying she wanted to use the loo and Mum told her that she was going to put on the kettle. They had been in a whole five minutes and no one had looked for me or thought that maybe I might want a snack.

I sat under the bed with my tail lashing. Then I heard Mum coming down the stairs.

'I haven't shown you the garden, have I Elaine?' she said.

Well that wouldn't take long!

Mum opened the door to the little courtyard and Elaine walked out. I decide to make myself visible to them and sit on the stairs.

'Kimmy!' said Mum.

Too late now, I thought. You hardly remembered you had me a moment ago. I decided to make a run for it.

Mum closed the doors to the garden and Elaine said she would just drink her tea and they'd set out again.

'There's still loads I want to see,' she said.

'We'll do another hour or two and then I'll drop you at the station after,' said Mum.

So she was going then? Not staying forever? Thank you!

Then I heard Mum say, 'Where's Kimmy?'

Ah, they'd noticed at last.

'She can't be far,' said Elaine as if she would know.

'Kimmy!' shouted Mum but I ignored it.'Kimmy!' again.

'Oh God!' said Mum, 'I hope she didn't run out to the garden while I had the door open. She could have shimmied up the wall and run off by now'.

'No. We'd have seen her,' said Elaine.

'No, we mightn't have done. I had the door open for a few moments before you came out of the loo. She might have slipped out then and I promised the Home I wouldn't let her out for at least two months …'

There was a long silence while they thought what to do next.

Elaine then offered to search everywhere. 'I'll do upstairs and you do downstairs,' she said. They both ran in opposite directions and I heard footsteps and bangs as they ran around.

Eventually, they met back in the kitchen.

'No luck?' asked Mum pointlessly.

'No,' admitted Elaine. 'But she can't be far.'

Mum made some sort of high pitched noise I didn't recognise.

'I'll go next door and see if she's slipped into their courtyard'.

I heard the door slam as Mum banged out. Elaine drank her tea nervously. Mum returned and said that no one had seen me.

'I tried the flats the other side. No luck!'

Mum called my name another few times and each time her voice got more panicked. I knew I should have shown myself then but I was keen to see how far she would go. And I have to admit I was beginning to nod off as it was warm and dark where I was.

'Look, Elaine. I am sorry but I don't think I can go shopping now'. Mum's voice trailed off.

'It's okay. It is time for me to be thinking of the train. I could get the earlier one if I dash'. Elaine's voice sounded less cheerful than it had earlier.

'Do you know what time the earlier one is?' asked Mum.

Elaine just shrugged.

'Oh, Elaine. You've come all this way ….!' Mum sounded upset.

I wondered how far London was.

Elaine gathered up her bags and pulled on her coat. Mum gave her a big hug and said sorry again.

'I just can't think where she's gone and I daren't go out in case she comes back. If she gets onto that road …'. They both looked towards the window and beyond.We all know what would happen on that road. The cars go past every few seconds and they were all very fast.

The door closed and Elaine was gone. Mum ran down the stairs again and opened the doors to the garden.

'Kimmy!' she called about a dozen times (I don't know as I can't count but it was a lot) but eventually I heard a man's voice coming from our neighbour's house calling out.

'Haven't you found her yet?'

'No I bloody well haven't. I'd hardly be calling out her name if I'd found her, now would I?'

'Well there's no *bloody* point shouting is there?'
The door slammed shut.

I'd never heard Mum sound so cross and I huddled down a bit to make myself even smaller. She was beginning to scare me. I began to lick my lips. This wasn't as much fun now. I might have let her see me then but after hearing how annoyed she was, I thought better of it.

She slammed up the stairs again and sank onto a chair by the table. I heard her talking into the little phone she carried with her because she can't fit the big one in her bag.

'Mum, it's me. I've lost Kimmy! ….. no, ages now. I think she must have got out'.

I listened.

'I've no idea Mum. And now Elaine has gone. Far earlier than planned. We hadn't even done the Guildhall Market… and I've fallen out with the neighbour to boot …'

I slumped even further down and decided that I would not come out while Mum was talking in this cross way about me. Her voice was all high and raised, she sounded very agitated.

'Yes, of course I've tried *EVERYWHERE*. Where else is there? Oh, I've got to go. She's gone. She hated me so much that she took the first chance to escape … that's how much she hates me'. Mum was rambling now. To my horror she began to make really funny noises and I recognised them as tears. Mum was crying. Crying because she thought she'd lost me! She put down her phone and ran to the cupboard under the sink where she pulled out a black plastic bag. 'Well, if I don't have a cat, then I won't need this.' And she began scraping my dinner into the bag and hurling my packets of food into the rubbish.

It was too much. She was getting rid of my food and she was upset too! I couldn't stay hidden for any longer this was going beyond a joke.

I pushed open the door of the cupboard under the sink where

Mum had been just a few moments ago and jumped out. Mum was kneeling on the floor, her face wet with tears. I rubbed myself up against her and purred nervously.

'Kimmy!' she shouted - but she wasn't cross with me, she was smiling and laughing and crying all at the same time.

'Oh God Kimmy! Is that where you've been? In the cupboard!' She picked me up and squeezed me until I could hardly breathe. I gave a pathetic little mew.

'Kimmy. I am *so* pleased to see you, you naughty cat'. She reached for her phone and began punching numbers into it and then I heard her saying.

'She's back! She's okay. She was just hiding in the cupboard under the sink'. She said this about ten times before she finally put down the phone and gave me some more dinner.

I did feel a bit bad now. Maybe I had gone a bit far. But three good things have come out of it. Mum hadn't spent any more money in the shops, Elaine had gone home - probably for good - and now I knew how much I was loved. That was pretty good for one day.

Chapter Five

Learning to Live Together

Monday 18th June

Mum and I had settled into a routine. I slept on her bed (which I now thought of as ours) and every morning I woke her up to feed me. This could be any time between dawn and when all the traffic outside is thundering past. Sometimes both.

After breakfast, I pestered Mum to let me out the double glass back doors *NEVER* the front door as I knew that would mean death. I liked to take a short walk around the courtyard-garden and get some fresh air. Sometimes I would do a little digging in the flower pots that were out there. Then I used my litter tray before it was time for my morning nap that I take on the bed downstairs (to give Mum time to tidy the one upstairs, I hated sleeping on a messy bed) or sometimes I curled up on the sofa. It depended on my mood and what was going on in the house. I liked it to be very quiet.

Then, around lunch-time, I'd have a little snack before retiring for my afternoon nap which is almost always on the bed at the top of the house. Next I had a light supper, watched some TV with my Mum before washing my face and a moonlight stroll in the garden. I may have done a little rolling around or perhaps chased a few toys - but nothing too strenuous. After that it was time for bed again. Exhausting.

I now knew how much Mum loved me and more to the point *she knew* how much she loved me. I heard her on the phone talking to her Mum.

'You see Mum, I had never realised how much Kimmy meant to me. I was thinking of what I had given up. My freedom - not being able to just go away on impulse and the responsibility. The awful smell of that food, her litter tray … all those types of things. If I'd lost her I thought I would just get over it … but then when I *really* thought she'd gone for good - I realised how much I loved her.

Ahhh … wasn't that sweet?

Top Tip

When sharing a bed with a human make sure that you get there first to ensure the most comfortable position (usually the top, middle, near the pillows). When your Mum gets in she will have to squeeze in around you. If you have to share with a Dad as well, this could be tricky – but make sure you don't end up with a tiny bit at the bottom of the mattress.

If you fail with the above and your family aren't suitable to be slept with – make sure that your own bed is as close to the radiator as possible.

Friday 22nd June

Mum made a huge fuss today and put extra effort into tidying the house. She even got out the vacuum cleaner and I knew she hated doing that as it meant moving lots of things that were in the way of the cupboard where she kept it. She told me that Jan from the Home was coming to visit again. All pets from there got another visit after a few months to see how they were getting on. Not to take me back surely? I remembered how I had hidden from Mum just the other day. I thought we had got over that. Maybe she was giving me back because I'd been naughty? Or perhaps the Home had heard that I had nearly run away and wanted to see if I was safe?

I heard the doorbell ring and I ran. Mum put away the polish and answered the door to let Jan in. Jan was tall and has some very red hair - not like Ginger's fur but a different colour although I don't really know colours. I think hers has been put in, if you see what I mean. She looked as if she'd been dipped in a pot of paint whereas Ginger's looked like he'd been born that way. She looked a bit 'wild' but was always smiling which made her eyes crinkle at the corners. She would always say something friendly to us at the new cattery. She talked about her own cats Cassie, Porsche and Mickey a lot. I can even smell them off her - three very distinct smells that made me feel as if I knew them. She was nice to me when she took my photo at the Home and I'd been told that she had done my home visit to decide if Mum was suitable. Now she was here possibly to take me back to that dingy cage. If Jan wanted to remove me from here she'd have to find me first! I burrowed deeper into my hiding place.

Jan and Mum sat at the kitchen table chatting for a while. Mum blew it because she didn't have anything for Jan to drink.

'Cordial?' asked Jan.

Mum shook her head. She only had wine, tea and coffee. I hoped that wouldn't make a difference to what Jan thought of her.

Jan agreed to a glass of water and I heard her tell Mum that she had seen Ginger the day before.

'Ginger?' enquired Mum.

'Yes, he was in the cage next to Kimmy's. Maybe you never met him. A big ginger cat?'

I wanted to scream out that I remembered him very well.

Mum shook her head. I knew she hadn't noticed him! She'd only had eyes for me.

'Well, he's okay. He's in a flat but has lots of other cat friends - on the estate. He's in a sort of gang ….'.

Mum didn't say much. I knew she was nervous.

Then I heard Jan ask how I'd been. 'She hasn't been going out has she?'

'No,' lied Mum. And then I worried that Jan had found out that I *had* been out and was here to punish me. Were my paw prints on the stairs and leading out to the garden? That would be a bit of a giveaway. Maybe someone had seen me and phoned the Home? I dug even deeper into my hiding place.

'Well, if I could just see her …,' said Jan after what seemed like forever.

And would you believe it? Mum only brought her over to the cupboard under the sink where I was hiding and opened the doors to reveal me sitting on a shelf at the back between the mugs and the washing powder! Oh no! I licked my lips and lashed my tail. How did she know?

'Ahhh,' said Jan. 'She's still timid'.

'Ah, yes,' said Mum shutting the doors, 'I suppose she is'.

Well, Jan didn't take me away and she told Mum that she had passed her home visit again.

So, I am being allowed to stay!

(Note from Kimmy's Mum; the Home do visit the pet again during the first few months but they really aren't there to take it away and wouldn't be able to without an extremely good reason anyway).

Wednesday 4th July

I was lying on my big warm bed having my afternoon nap when my Mum came running up the stairs and into the room. She was laughing and threw herself down beside me so I had to wake up and listen to her. I blinked.

'Kimmy, I've just been to Larkhall on my bike and guess what happened?'

I'm a cat! How could I possibly guess what happened when Mum goes off on one of her trips. I could see that Mum was bursting to tell me.

'I went to the pet shop to buy you … you know, your food'.

My ears pricked up. I knew the word 'food'.

'I saw this poster in the window with a photo of a cat and I thought, how lovely. It was one of those 'Can you give a cat a good home?' posters. It was the most beautiful cat and then I thought … hey, that looks familiar …'

I yawned. Mum's stories can go on forever.

'And it was you! Kimmy it was you on a poster in Larkhall! Okay so the poster was old but you had been chosen for National Pet Week and I fell for you all over again'.

I stared at her, not quite sure what to do. But she hadn't finished.

'It had your name on it and everything, 'Kimmy!'

I purred. I was known far and wide in Bath.

'So I went in and told the lady in the shop that you were mine and that you weren't looking for a home any more'.

I rolled over onto my back to show off my tummy.

'The lady in the shop wrote a little note saying, 'Re-homed to a lovely lady in Bath' and she stuck it on the poster in the window. Do you hear me Kimmy? She said 'lovely'.

I stared back at her and thought how easy it was to please humans.

Top Tip

When your Mum is telling you a boring story (and perhaps if you don't understand much human) try not to yawn. Instead stare at her as if fascinated but keep your mind fixed on what you might be having for dinner.

Wednesday 11th July

I thought I had discovered a way to stop Mum disturbing me when I was sleeping. I lay on my back with my paws over my eyes and that should let her know that I do not WANT TO BE DISTURBED. Unfortunately she didn't know that was what I meant and she stroked me. So I scratched her with my paw and that let her know! Okay so it's mean but sometimes a cat has to do what a cat has to do.

Chapter Six

The Cat Feeder

Friday 13th July

Mum was up to something but I don't know what. She kept making an enormous fuss of me (which is good) but she was getting all tearful when she talked to me (and that was bad). She had been busy putting clothes into a small bag but I didn't know what that meant. I thought I had come across this before but I couldn't remember. What did it mean if your carer started packing clothes? I watched everything she did very carefully but eventually she gave me a huge hug and I heard the front door bang closed.

Good, a bit of peace at last. I carried on with my morning nap that soon became my afternoon nap. When I woke up I noticed that the house was still very quiet. Mum hadn't come back!

I padded down the stairs to my food bowl and found it empty and I started to panic. But then I heard a key in the lock and the relief made me roll over with joy.

But the lady who came in was not my Mum – she was someone else. She was that 'pet feeder' from all those weeks ago. She must have passed her interview. Now she was staring down at me as I lay with my legs akimbo.Oh no!

I decided to do a runner. I didn't like the pet feeder and wanted my own Mum back. I ran and ran until I reached the cupboards under the phone that Mum was always talking on. There was a shelf in there with a hollow bit underneath. A cat like me could squeeze in and be hidden at the back. No human could reach me. I lay there with my heart jumping around inside me.

I waited till I heard the door slam closed as she left and I slowly came back down again. This time I found my food bowl full and I gingerly started to eat.

Supper over, I went upstairs for what should be TV watching but instead the box thing wasn't on and Mum's chair was empty. I sat and stared at the screen, like Mum does, but couldn't see the attraction. Then I prowled about like a wild feral cat and not the scaredey cat that I was feeling. I looked for anything that might frighten me but mostly I looked for monsters - giant mice or rats. Then, at last, I climbed upstairs to bed and hoped that I wouldn't have to spend the whole night on my own as I am scared of the dark. There was plenty of room on the bed but I felt very lonely and eventually I crawled under it and hid.

Saturday 14- Sunday15th July

Would you believe it but my Mum still hadn't come home. I was all alone in this big house which at night time is very dark and lonely. I had no one to brush me or to notice every little thing I did. This is *so* the opposite of being spoilt. I had been left 'home alone'.

The pet feeder lady came and cleaned my plates and emptied out my litter tray. She put far too much litter in it so I have to dig really hard. The food was okay but she just put it down and left it so I didn't get to do my 'I hate this food' routine. Nor did she watch to see if I had enjoyed it, like Mum does. She put a lot in my plate so that it doesn't run out but I don't like too much all at once. Most cats prefer dainty portions followed by another dainty portion. But she spoke my name very gently and I supposed she was doing her best. A few minutes after she'd arrived, I heard the door slam. She'd left.

Top Tip

Whiskas, Felix and even gourmet ranges are all well and good – delicious even – but a truly pampered cat will aspire to food that has to be specially ordered from a pet shop at huge expense to your Mum.

It should go without saying that own-brand cat-food is *never* acceptable under any circumstances.

Don't accept any of that nonsense about hunting birds or mice for our own meals. When was the last time you saw your family going off with a gun or a fishing rod to get something to put in a sandwich? No, if it doesn't come from a shop don't eat it.

Monday 16th July

Just as I was getting used to having the whole house to myself and having the pet feeder, to look after me, I heard the front door open and someone running up the stairs. I jumped to my four paws and began to arch my back in fierce cat mode. I was all ready to hiss and spit to protect my territory.

I knew immediately I heard two steps on the stairs that it was Mum – we just do don't we? I decided to pretend to ignore her for a while to show utter disgust at what she had done. Leaving me alone like that! But when she started to look upset I decided I'd gone too far and I started to purr and lick her hand. Then I rolled over and showed her my tummy. She picked me up and carried me downstairs where she scraped the old dinner into the bin and gave me a fresh one and sat with me, watching me while I ate it.

I was quite surprised to admit how pleased I was to see my Mum back. The house has been very quiet without her. Purrrrrrrr.

Top Tip

If your Mum goes away and you are left on your own, use the time to catch up on any personal grooming. This could entail sharpening nails on furniture or digging claws into carpets. Either way you get a perfect manicure without your Mum shouting at you.

Chapter Seven

Getting Seriously Spoiled

Tuesday 17th July

Mum brought me back a lovely big cushion that looked like a ladybird. She said that her mother (my granny?) had bought it for me and I heartily approved of getting expensive and comfortable presents. I spent the day lying on it and purring while Mum took photos of me.

Saturday 21st July

It had been very wet and stormy during the night and I slept badly. We were all told to 'stay indoors' if we could so I was surprised to see Mum getting ready to go out. Weeks ago she had suggested that she could make a better job of being a home visitor and now she had been taken seriously. Today she was off to do a course to learn how. I can't believe that they actually *teach* people these things! A home has to be very comfortable with excellent regular meals and people who adore the pet. How easy was that? Still, off she went and I was left all alone again. She came back late so I missed lunch and had to just have an early supper instead. She was in quite a good mood. I think she was quite looking forward to looking inside people's houses and I was happy to lend her for that job.

Wednesday 1st August

Sometimes I think I have the best Mum in the whole world! Ever since I moved in we've had a certain 'morning routine'. I wake up starving hungry. I pad downstairs to see what food I can find. Sometimes I have left a little of my supper behind and other times, I eat a little dried food that is always left out for me (I hate it). After I have done this I pay a little visit to my cat litter tray and then decide that I am still hungry. Mum is, of course, still asleep through all this because she's pretty lazy.

I then go back upstairs and have had to wake her at what she calls 'dawn' but what I call 'breakfast time'. I couldn't help it. I just got hungry and had to eat. I usually jumped up on top of her as she slept and purred and brushed myself around her. Sometimes I would lick or bite her, like I do when I am grooming. If it is good enough for me, she must like it too. Occasionally she pulled her big bedcovers over her and tried to hide from me but I lifted up my paw and pulled it back. If this didn't work I did something very clever. I jumped up at the wooden curtains and pushed myself against them so that one opens a little bit. Then I hooked my paw in and pulled. Hey presto! Daylight filled the room. I then heard Mum groan but soon after she was shuffling into her woollen shoes and trailing behind me down to where she kept the food. I patted that door too to help her open it and then I pushed it right back so she can really see what is in there.

Occasionally she got up during the night to use her own litter tray in the bathroom and I followed her in, crying urgently for food. But usually she just crawled back into bed – or if I was very lucky she followed me downstairs to the kitchen. Mum said she had been doing this every day for 'months' now and was getting very tired. So, today she set out to the pet shop and came back with a special present. It was a dish with a lid. I hope she didn't expect me to get excited. She had done something to it so it showed the time and then when five o'clock in the morning came – the lid opened and inside was my breakfast! I didn't have to wake Mum any more and I got a nice full tummy when I was hungry. All I had to do was wait by the box and it sprung up to reveal its delicious contents. This was brilliant and truly showed that she loved me. I heard her on the phone to her mother and she was saying, 'I don't care what it cost, Mum, now at least I can get a full night's sleep'.

So you see, everyone is happy!

Top Tip

If your Mum fails to wake when you bite and paw her face, try some loud mewing. If that fails (and you aren't able to open the blinds, curtains or wooden shutters) press your bottom into her face. That should do the trick. If all else fails (and this is desperate measures), start scratching the carpet just outside her bedroom door. That will get her up even if she is a bit cross with you.

Friday 3rd August

Mum came down during the night to get a glass of water. I think she'd been at that funny red drink that makes her laugh a lot. That always seems to make her thirsty even though she has drunk a lot already. I was sitting at the new dish with the lid and Mum asked what I was doing. Then, a miracle! The lid popped up and there was the food. I began to tuck in hungrily. Mum seemed very amused.

'Kimmy you knew it was 5 am! How do you do that?' marvelled Mum as she shuffled off back upstairs to bed.

How does she think I knew the time?! I just knew that I was hungry and that was when I should get my breakfast.

After I had eaten it, I went back upstairs again. I saw that Mum had gone back to sleep but I wanted to show her how grateful I was. So, I jumped on top of her and purred my appreciation.

'Oh Kimmy,' she said rolling over and taking the duvet with her. 'You've woken me up again …' and then I heard her snoring.

Sunday 5th August

Mum overslept and blamed me for not waking her! A cat can never win, can she?

Chapter Eight

The Vet

Friday 10th August

This was the worst day since I moved here. I woke with a sore ear and was shaking my head a bit to try and clear it. Mum was watching me and looking worried.

'Kimmy is your ear painful? Let me see?' she asked. I didn't reply as I didn't like her trying to peer inside it either. Mum got all clingy and silly, her face all wrinkled into a mass of frowns.

I went upstairs for my morning nap but the next thing I knew Mum was gently scooping me up in her arms and carrying me down the stairs and she *never* did that. Usually she shoos me as she walked behind or she just called me. But now she was carrying me as if I was very sick or too old to walk. And the next thing I saw was that dreaded carrying box that I haven't seen since I moved in here. It was open at the front and standing on its side. It was what I was carried in when I came in to this house and every single time I go in it, apart from then, meant something bad or uncertain happens. I would *not* go in that box! I began to struggle and kick and I even tried to scratch her but she was stronger and she forced me inside and then closed the lid. It felt very cruel and nasty and totally mean from someone who I thought loved me. I lay there with my heart beating so fast I thought it would jump right out of the cage like one of those frog-things that I used to see near my old home. What had I done wrong? I thought she loved me! I wanted to tell her that if she didn't take me where she is going to take me I would promise never to scratch the carpet again. But she only spoke a little cat and couldn't understand me, although usually we are both quite good at communicating. I sank back into the box thinking about what to do.

Then I saw the door opening. This is the big one at the front of the house - not like the glass ones that lead out to the garden in the basement. It went out to the noisy street beyond. I was not allowed near this door - not even to look at it. Once I was sitting on the stair when Mum came in and she screamed and told me to go away and slammed the door shut until I had done what she asked. I don't know what it is about that door but when it was open the house was filled with a terrible racket and I wanted to cover my ears. Nasty dirty fumes and dust blew in and I knew that even if Mum let me go out that way, I never would. Now she was carrying me out to the danger beyond. I felt the cold air in my fur and I was even more scared. This was a big busy road! Mum put a thick towel over my cage and I felt a little better. I couldn't see now – only smell (and that's bad enough). I wondered where she was taking me and really hoped she was not bringing me back to the Home. I would hate to go back there even though they were nice to me. I started to cry again.

She walked and walked for what seemed like forever and I could see a little of the bottom of people's legs through a gap in the towel as we walked past them. She was swinging me a bit – back and forward and I felt a little sick. Then I was carried in through another door that

Mum pushed open and found myself in a warm, quieter room. Then she set my box down. The towel slipped off and I could see around me. A big dog was about a paw's length away from me, sniffing at my cage. A cat was in a carrier nearby. She *was* taking me back to the Home! I'd seen that happen. Cats would go out and then a few days later they'd be back. I must have done something wrong. *What?*

I heard her speaking to someone. 'She's called Kimmy … yes, a sore ear.'

I was carried over to another bit of the room and this time I could see everything. There were about three dogs in the room and some other cats. We were all crying and it just added to my misery. This was just like the Home when I was brought in. I looked at Mum and she was reading a magazine. So, she didn't even care! A few dogs went in and came out again. Then they left through the door we had come in by. Perhaps they were being taken out and put in the big cages that they had at the Home? After what seemed like a very long time, a man came out of another room and called out my name, 'Kimmy!' How did he know? Was I so famous in Bath that everyone knew me?

Mum picked up my box and carried me into the room and set me down on a table. The man (who I didn't know) opened the front of the carrier and to my horror he tried to get me out. I stiffened and he gently tipped me forward. I fell out. The man stroked me and I sensed that he was nice. He was certainly gentle, but I was beginning to recognise where I might be. This was a vet! I knew vets I had seen them before - they all wore those coats. I thought of the big injection that Ginger had told me about. The big injection that makes you go to sleep *forever.*

Mum told him that I seemed to have a sore ear and he reached forward to look. I felt strong arms around me holding me tightly. It hurt when he put something in it and then pulled it out. Ouch …! Then I felt something wet and sticky being dropped in and he pressed on my ear. Okay was that it? But Mum was saying something else. They both hold me very firmly and he opened my mouth and peered in. I was not sure what he said next but Mum looked very upset and I started to panic again. He asked her what I have eaten that day.

'Er, just her 5 am breakfast and then another, um, breakfast at about 8. But she didn't finish the later one. That's what let me know that she couldn't be well …'. He looked at her and shook his head.

So? What's wrong with that? I had a healthy appetite. I wanted to remind him I hadn't even finished my second breakfast and barely touched the first one!

'I can do it this afternoon,' he told Mum.

Do what?

Then another woman came in and took me in my basket from Mum and she walked away with me! No, she *was* leaving me behind. It was like being at the Home all over again. I heard Mum leaving and closing the door behind. 'Goodbye Kimmy,' she said.

'Please take me with you!'

I was put in a dark room where the vet was coming towards me with *A BIG NEEDLE …. Z*

The next thing I knew I was being picked up and put back in my carrier again. This time Mum was there, her face all smiles. Then after giving them her card-thing that she paid for things with, she left the room with me. We were back out onto the street again with the nasty smells and the terrible loud noises. When I breathed nasty, dirty stuff went up my nose. But I didn't care! Mum had come back for me and for some reason whatever was in that needle made me feel all sleepy and relaxed.

We walked the way we had come before but this time I wasn't so worried. Then Mum opened the door to the house and suddenly I was back in my familiar room again. Everything looked just the same. I had had this life changing experience but nothing in my home was any different.

Mum stooped down beside me. 'Are you okay Kimmy? You had your teeth and gums cleaned. Do you feel okay?. Was the vet nice to you? I've been worrying all day'.

All day! Had I been gone that long? But what I didn't understand was why when a cat goes in with a sore ear, she ended up having her mouth cleaned. It makes no sense at all but I felt very strange, sort of relaxed and happy but a bit wobbly and tired. I was happy to let Mum pick me up again and she carried me upstairs. She put me on her big warm bed and I snuggled into the pillows and drifted off back into a deep sleep. Zzzzzzzzzzzzzzzzzzz.

I was still sleeping when Mum gently moved me and squeezed into the bed herself.

Zzzzzzzzzzzzzzzzzzz.

Saturday 11th August

I didn't wake up once until this morning. I went for a celebratory furniture-scratching session but discovered I had no nails left. Someone has cut them right down. It must have been while I was asleep at the vet's. Is there no end of humiliation for a cat to bear?

Later on I saw Mum asleep on the sofa. She liked to have a nap sometimes when she should be working. I jumped up beside her and lay along her chest - which was where I liked to be. I loved Mum best when she was sleeping as she was less noisy and I could cuddle up to her and get all snugly.

Top Tip

When your Mum is reading a newspaper make sure that you sit on it to stop her seeing the pages. She will expect it and be disappointed if you don't.

Chapter Nine

Home Alone

Friday 17th – Monday 20th August

Mum went away again and left me all alone. Can you believe it? I was only home from the vet's a few days after emergency surgery. ***(Note from Kimmy's Mum; she had her teeth cleaned ...)*** I wish she wouldn't do that as I get quite scared and I don't get enough to eat. My cat feeder came round and filled my bowl up but it is not the same. I am still a little frightened of her as I don't really know her. I went to my secret hiding place - a cupboard with shelves in the drawing room. I could just about squeeze myself into the cupboard and down and underneath one of the wooden slats so I couldn't be seen. This made me feel very safe. The neighbours were making a lot of noise and this made me even more nervous. I heard her calling out my name from downstairs in the kitchen but I was too fast for her and I hurried into my cubby hole. Unfortunately I couldn't pull the door shut behind me so I think she must have guessed where I was because I heard her speak to the closed doors. 'Bye Kimmy'.

Then one night well after bedtime, I was under the bed because that's another place where I feel safe. I heard the door bang downstairs and then footsteps coming fast up the stairs. I froze and realised that I didn't have enough time to run to my hiding place, as I would pass the intruder on the stairs. My body went all stiff, like it did when I don't like what was happening. Oh no! I'm too young to die - I'm only ten! I tried not to breathe and stayed very still hoping then that maybe the person won't find me. Would a burglar bother with a little cat like me? A head bobbed under the bed all crinkled because it was upside down. I knew my Mum even when she was the wrong way up!

'Mum!' I mewed.

'Kimmy,' she cried.

For the next ten minutes I licked and pawed her like I'd seen dogs do. I was just so pleased to see her. She stroked and kissed me and seemed as happy to see me as I was to see her. I snuggled down feeling safe and warm again - but not before Mum gave me my favourite supper of chicken slices. I went to sleep that night a very happy cat.

Top Tip

If your Mum has to go away and isn't able to take you with her, make sure that she buys you a Feliway. This plugs into the wall and lets off special scents that calms us cats when life gets stressful. You should be able to get them at the vet's or Bath Cats and Dogs Home sell them.

Monday 27th August

The trouble about Mum going away was that every time she went out I worried that maybe she wasn't going to come back. Tonight she got all dressed up and I heard the door close behind her. It got late and dark and just when I had given up hope, she came home. I ignored her for a while to show I was cross and then I jumped up on the bed and made a huge fuss of her. I couldn't pretend to be cross with her for long!

Chapter Ten

The Heiress

Wednesday 29th August

Mum has been fretting that Auntie Jan's cats, Mickey, Porsche and Cassie might be more spoilt than me - especially as Porsche goes to a special grooming salon. But she came up with a plan to out-do her. She told some legal people on the phone that she wanted to re-write her will. She wanted to write me into it! She told me that every cat should be provided for 'just in case'. I am not quite sure what a will is or why I need to be provided for but I did realise that if anything bad should happen to Mum, I would be okay and not have to go back into that Home again and I've seen the way she rides her bicycle so I think she was right to think of these things. Mum was trying to work out how much I cost her so she knew how much to leave. She sat at the table writing down, Whiskas twice a day er, three times and then multiplied by seven and then fifty two. But eventually she just said, 'Oh Kimmy, it is so difficult,' and she told me she has left me enough to be cared for. 'It's enough,' was all she'd say, mysteriously. I didn't want to think what life would be like without Mum but I liked the idea of being rich. Mum told me that officially I was now 'an heiress'. I liked the sound of that! I thought of Ginger and wondered if he had an ASBO yet?

Auntie Jan was suitably impressed when she heard. She had only been *thinking* of doing this but hadn't actually got round to it.

So, that is one up to Kimmy!

Top Tip

Make sure that your Mum (or Dad if you have one) makes you rich when they die. If they can't leave you rich make sure they leave you 'enough'. They don't have to be rich to make arrangements for you if 'anything' should happen. You will be very sad to be left alone but at least you'll not starve – or worse still end up at Bath Cats and Dogs Home (again). No offence. Or get them to check out the RSPCA's Home for Life Scheme.

Chapter Eleven

The Rough with the Smooth

Friday 31st August

Something very strange had happened. I went down to use my loo this morning and it wasn't there ... it was inside the bathroom. Mum had been putting a second box in there for a while now but I got used to using the one in the hall and why break a habit? Okay so it was not that private but so far, it has worked. Now I had the confusing experience of having to choose which one of the two to use. I asked myself, 'What would a truly spoilt cat do?' And it came to me! *I will use both.* Every cat has two er, different reasons to use their toilet and why mix the boxes up - especially as Mum had given me lovely soft paper in one of them and good gritty cat lit in the other? It was so fantastic! I had two loos all to myself. Who wanted to get into a tray that is already wet or smells of pee? (Although my Mum (naturally) cleared mine out twice a day).

(Note from Kimmy's Mum; the two boxes started because I wanted to encourage her to use the downstairs bathroom rather than do her business in the hall. I was going to get her to use one then I would get rid of the other. I used two different types of cat lit because the

paper litter is lighter to carry and I'd run out of the usual. It turned out that cat experts (Celia Hadden, Weekend Telegraph although now she has retired) said that all cats should have two boxes if possible. And put newspaper underneath each tray as they love a good scratch after to get rid of the cat lit and to simulate burying their waste.)

Sunday 2nd September

Mum got up and went out early because she said she was helping out at Bath Cats and Dogs Home Open Day. This was when they put up lots of tents selling things to people and then all the money would go towards the Home. They put Mum in the Shrinks' Think Tank where they had Dr Roger Mugford, (a pet psychologist would you believe? He was a dog doctor!) and someone called Sarah Fisher who knew about Touch Therapy. Mum said she asked questions about *me* and that Dr Mugford said that cats were too perfect to need psychologists! (That's true). And Sarah told her that cats love having their ears rubbed as this calms them and brings down their blood pressure. Mum came home tired but excited and gently rubbed my ears for ages and ages and I felt wonderful at the end. It really helped me sleep well and I felt thoroughly spoilt.

I was pleased to hear that the day had gone well and that the Home made over £30,000. It costs nearly £3,000 a day to run the home so this will be good for 10 days. Looking back, it now seemed a long time ago that I was there. I like to think that I had forgotten it now. I really have moved on.

Mum went all quiet and thoughtful and then said, 'Maybe we could write something about you, Kimmy, and make some money for the Home. They really need it.'

I purred my approval. Anything about me *had* to be worth doing.

Monday 3rd - Wednesday - 5th September

Mum got up far earlier than usual and gave me my second breakfast (I have my first at 5 am). I knew something was up because she didn't normally do this. The next thing I knew I was carried upstairs and then I heard the bedroom door close behind me. She never did this either. I was to be shut in *all day*. Some men came and they started banging and I heard the most dreadful noises you could ever imagine. Scraping and drilling. The sort of noise that makes your teeth hurt. And over the top of that they had music on so it all sounded *terrible*. I just wanted to stuff my paws into my ears and make it all go away. I started to cry and finally Mum came up to see me but I was right in the back of her wardrobe with some of her clothes pulled around my head. I was trying to get my head to fit inside one of her shoes.

'I know Kimmy. It is awful,' she said as the pictures on the wall rattled.

It was so bad that Mum went out and I heard the door slam behind her. Later on when it had all gone quiet and I heard the men shout goodbyes and banged the door closed, she coaxed me out of my hiding place. 'They've left now, Kimmy,' she said.

Pardon? I was now deaf! But a good supper would make me feel a little better.

Later on I went downstairs to the basement to see what they had done. I still feel upset telling this. The staircase, hall and little bedroom with the people's feet that walk past was full of the most dreadful dust and this horrible nasty black stuff coated all the walls. There were big plastic sheets hanging over the doorways, like bags. And it smelt *terrible*. What had they done to my beautiful house? Why had Mum let them? Who could have done such a thing?

I screamed and ran off and hid back in the cupboard. Mum pulled open the door and peered in.

'I know Kimmy, it's a dreadful mess. I'd be right in there with you if I could fit.'

It turned out that she had had a little bit of damp in the basement and had allowed these men to take off all the outside layer of wall and put some yucky stuff on to keep out the water.

I'd rather have had the water.

Wednesday 5th September

The men finally left and the house was quiet again although it still looked a mess. I hoped that Mum would clear it up. To celebrate the return to peace and quiet I let her brush me until my fur gleamed. I felt happy again.

I thought Mum was happy again too as I heard her tapping away on her laptop. She was writing about Sunday's Shrink Think Tank for the Home. I thought it was for Jan – or Auntie Jan as I was now to call her. Later when I heard her on the phone telling her Mum how scared I'd been she'd said, 'Kimmy has a pretty good life. She will just have to take the rough with the smooth.' Charming!

Wednesday 12th September

I now had my own patch of lawn to eat if I felt like it. Mum had grown me some grass in a box that sits on the window seat. I could eat it without going out. I liked this as it was like salad for cats!

Top Tip

If you don't have a garden (like Ginger) make sure that your Mum grows you some grass to eat as it is useful roughage and may stop you getting hair balls. You can throw it up again later when Mum's watching TV.

Chapter Twelve

Nurse Kimmy

Friday 14th September

I had found a new place to nap … Mum's chair where she liked to sit. I used it for my afternoon nap. Tonight Mum sat there to watch that TV thing and I tried to stare her out so she'd give it back to me but she ignored me. When she got up to get something from downstairs I jumped onto the seat so when she came back she had to sit on the other chair – the one she doesn't like as much … Result!

Saturday 22nd - Sunday23rd September

Mum wasn't feeling very well. She'd been a bit wheezy from all the dust in the house and had gone running but came back saying that she'd hurt her ankle now as well. I'm not sure how having a wheeze can end up hurting your ankle but it did. She was in such pain that she had to hobble everywhere. She had also been to the dentist and they'd been mean to her about her teeth (now she knew how I felt when I went to the vet only her teeth are going to cost a lot more than mine did). She'd been told that she needed some crowns replacing and it would cost a lot to put them right. She was so upset that she said she was going to bed. Luckily she could still get down the stairs to feed me but she was full of pain- killers. She was feeling very sorry for herself and did look very pale. She said that it had just hit her that she was living in a strange city where she didn't know people and was suddenly feeling homesick and vulnerable, whatever that is.

'I moved here because it felt lucky, Kimmy. And now – that damp problem, my ankle and teeth ….'. She looked pretty miserable.

She decided to stay in bed with some magazines and a book. 'I need TLC Kimmy,' she told me. So I, Kimmy, took it upon myself to be a very good nurse. I stayed with Mum on the bed purring and snuggling up close to her. I wanted her to know that even though her life seemed very bad indeed she could be sure that I would still love her. After a few days, she got up and said she felt a bit better. That's the power of having a cat to nurse you.

(Note from Kimmy's Mum; I was feeling horrible that weekend. I had Achilles Tendonitis and my heel/ankle was very sore. I'd also been told I needed loads of expensive dental work. I felt as if my body had really let me down but having a cat is better than a nurse. Stroking a cat lowers the blood pressure and just having her there made me feel two hundred times better.)

Top Tip

If your Mum is not well make sure that you stay with her and make a big fuss. She will adore you for it and it is a good excuse for staying in bed all day and being extra lazy.

Chapter Thirteen

Pet Insurance

Monday 1st October

Mum started to fix some of the things that the workmen had damaged when they were in a few weeks ago. She'd been told to wait a few weeks and today she painted the wooden stairs. I watched carefully while she painted from the bottom right up to the top and then I decided to walk down. Mum screamed at me but I was clever and walked around the bits of paint. She looked on in amazement. Did she really think that I would want to get sticky white stuff on my paws?

Tuesday 2nd October

Mum came home all excited from the pet shop because she had bought me some dried food that came with a FREE tent. Or to be more precise it was a tent that came with some very expensive food that I wasn't going to eat. It was a curious looking thing shaped like a triangle with a little door at the front. She pulled it out of its plastic bag and tried to get me to go in it. As if?! She seemed to think that me in something that was used for outdoor camping was very funny and I heard her on the phone to Auntie Jan. Every time one of them said the word 'tent' or the word 'camping' the other one burst out laughing.

'She could go camping in the Lake District - with Mickey,' snorted Mum (Mickey was Auntie Jan's cat and officially 'my boyfriend'. He is black and white and very gorgeous …).

I couldn't make out everything they were saying as they were laughing so much but I made up my mind that I wouldn't *ever* be seen in this plastic-nylon contraption if it made Mum behave so oddly. I yawned and went upstairs for my afternoon nap just as I heard Mum say, 'They could go *camping* in the Cotswolds!'

Needless to say I never set paw in the tent.

Thursday 4th October

Mum went to do a post home visit – that's when they've already got the pet and she goes to see if it is okay - like Jan did for me. Usually she comes home all gooey and smelling of cat but today she seemed very upset. 'Oh Kimmy,' she said swooping on me dramatically and squashing me. I felt big hot tears falling into my fur and I wondered what was wrong.

I heard her on the phone talking to the Home a bit later. It turned out that the man who she had said was okay to have a cat had lied to her. He had told her that he had a job. But today she learned that he hadn't and she thought his flat was uncomfortable.

'But June,' she was saying, (does everyone at the Home have names beginning with J?) 'he's on benefits and he can't afford to heat his flat!'

I gulped deeply and understood why Mum was so upset. Cats love to be warm and comfortable. If Mum suddenly got poor and couldn't afford heating, I'd have to think again about loving her.

'He *did* say he had a job'.

I thought of Mum and the minutes she spent on the laptop and the words 'pot, kettle and black' came to mind.

'But when I went back today he told me he is on benefits and he'd even tried to get free veterinary care'.

This man's poor cat has some sort of bad illness that is so bad he can't have the pet insurance that I have (you get this automatically if you come from the Home and it is free for a while. Then you have to pay it yourself or cancel it). Because he had no job he can't afford to pay for a vet.

If I'd been Mum I'd have asked to see his bank manager. We cats can't have enough luxury and a flat is bad enough but one that has no heating? I shuddered. I wouldn't wish that on even Ginger! I could just cry for him – even if I did envy him not having to go to the vet. I had to go there all the time. Maybe he could go instead of me.

Mum came off the phone and hugged me again and I purred to show my appreciation. Once again, I was glad I'd chosen her.

Top Tip

Make sure that your Mum can afford to pay for pet insurance – which could be about £10 a month. Even though we hate going to the vet's we need to know that they can afford to pay for us if we get sick. You don't have to be rich to own a cat but you do need to be able to afford food and vet's bills.

Chapter Fourteen

More Spoiling

Monday 9th October

I tried the water in my bowl and do you know what? Mum had poured it from a jug she'd taken from the fridge but it wasn't just cold - it had a different taste. It tasted of nothing! No nasty after taste in my mouth. Delicious. I drank lots.

(Note from Kimmy's Mum; I bought a water filter because I had heard that cats have a much stronger sense of smell than we do. While we all know that our tap water is safe to drink we also know that sometimes it is a bit smelly. Think what that's like for a cat. A filter cleans out the nasties and makes a cat drink more of it. You can also use rain water that you collect from the garden although I used tap water.)

Thursday 11th October

Once again I have the best Mum ever ...! She went to a huge store in Bristol with a funny sounding foreign name (you know the ones who were always advertising their sale on the telly?) She bought lots of stuff which she said was all very cheap. She came back with lovely fresh bed linen. She had also bought an electric blanket a few days before but today she put it on along with the fresh sheets and duvet cover. So I jumped on for a nap and now I was really toastie. It is very important for cats to have all the comforts and this was just purrfection … purr.

Mum also wrote to that Chronic paper that she's always reading – the one that is local to Bath. I was in it once when I was 'Pet of the Month'. She asked people to give money for the Home because they seem to need it even more than usual. Her letter went in today. It had a nice big photo, not of me, but of some celeb and a dog. Why was that – why wasn't it me?

She told me that she was entering me in a photo competition at the Home and I heard her telling Auntie Jan that she was going to put five photos in. This means I would have no peace for the next week or more while she followed me around with her camera. But right now I was so relaxed lying on her lovely clean bed that I don't care. Then she had to spoil it all by sneaking up on me and dropping those nasty, sticky wet drops from a little plastic bottle into my ear. They were the ones that the vet had given her. Ugh.

My Granny was coming over the following week (that's the lady who was with Mum when she first saw me at the Home all those weeks ago). I hoped I would get really spoilt rotten as I deserved to be. I was also expecting her to bring me presents. But now it was time for Mum to give me a brushing. We must take care of the grooming; a spoilt cat can never let herself go.

Friday 12th October

Mum bought a new silk bedspread for the spare room downstairs. This was beyond bliss … me lying on silk? *Purrfection … puuuuuuuuuurrrrrrrrrr*

Chapter Fifteen

A *Slightly* Sore Throat

Saturday 13th October

I didn't fancy my breakfast this morning. I didn't know why. Maybe I was getting tired of Whiskas - although I never thought that I would say that - and would like to try something different. I gave Mum one of my looks and she immediately opened a can of tuna but I didn't really like that either. I was really holding out for some fresh chicken but much to my horror I was back in my carrying box again and off to see my the vet. To say I over-played my hand was an understatement! If I could have had that plate of tuna back I'd wolf it down now.

The waiting room was far fuller than when we went before and there were lots of dogs barking and a cat looking suspiciously like Ginger was in a box next to mine. He looked happy so I knew it couldn't be my old enemy. I hissed at him just in case. We had to sit there for *ages* until my name was called.

'Kimmy please'.

Mum picked my carrier up and lifted me into the surgery where I was gently tipped onto the table. I began to cry, naturally.

'Well?' asked the vet curiously.

'She skipped breakfast,' said Mum.

The vet's eyebrow shot upwards and I tried to escape downwards but two pairs of strong hands held me.

The next thing I knew my mouth was being forced open and something was shoved down it. Then one of those nasty things was being shoved up my bottom. What would they do to me next?

'Hmmmmm,' said the vet.

'Yes?' asked Mum, looking like she was going to cry again.

'I think that Kimmy has a slightly sore throat'.

'Slightly?'

'Yes. Nothing serious.' Then he jabbed one of those dreaded needles into me. Not the *needle*? Were they going to kill me because I had a slightly sore throat?

'Some antibiotics,' said the vet, putting me back in my box. I was still alive.

'That'll be £32.00 please,' said the smiling nurse as we left.

The next thing I knew I was being carried across the road with Mum muttering, '£32 for a *slightly* sore throat.'

I was starving when I got in and stuffed myself with all the food that had been put down for me earlier.

'£32,' muttered Mum for the rest of the day.

I thought she'd be pleased I was okay?

Top Tip

Don't pull the 'I don't feel like eating that' stunt too often or you'll end up at the vet. But make sure that you have your Flu booster up to date.

Monday 15th October

Mum and I were both sneezing like mad. I think we had colds but this time, I was not being taken to the vet. My nose felt sore and runny. Drops of moisture kept falling from it. There was just one consolation - Mum's nose looked big and red. At least I didn't look like that. So you see I wasn't bluffing. I really was sick!

Chapter Sixteen

Mum's Revenge

Tuesday October 16th

I heard Mum on the phone to the Home (it now seemed *so* long ago since I was there). I lay on my velvet cushion and listened in. It turned out she had seen a woman a few weeks before who had fallen for a kitten on open day. They don't usually let the public just see kittens unless they've been visited because kittens are so cute that if anyone sees one they automatically want one and not everyone is suitable - if they live on a busy road or are out a lot. Mum had gone to her home and thought she was okay although dafter than most and that her house and garden were fantastic for a cat - safe. It had turned out that the woman returned the kitten just a few days later saying that the kitten was sick - when it wasn't. It just had a bit of diarrhoea that lots of cats get when they are given too much milk or are nervous. I felt like crying when I heard this as I tried to imagine how I would have felt if someone had taken me from the Home to a new warm and cosy home and returned me to a cold cage. How Ginger would have laughed (had he been there). Mum was upset too and I heard her say that she might give up being a Home Visitor if this was how bad her judgement was. I hoped she wouldn't as I knew that she really did care and I'd like to think I had some part in finding other cats a really good home, like mine – even if it was just sharing my Mum with them.

The woman who had returned the cat worked in a well-known American clothes store on the high street. Mum set off to go and I heard the door slam as she left. When she returned she told me that she had gone into the shop and tried on everything they sold in her size in the tiny changing rooms. She even sent the woman off to get her different sizes. Then she left them all behind for the nasty lady to put away! She told me she felt a lot better afterwards and I got an extra cuddle that night.

(Note from Kimmy's Mum; if you want to get a kitten, think very hard about what this will mean to your lifestyle BEFORE taking it home with you.)

Chapter Seventeen

Granny Comes to Stay

Thursday 18th October

My Granny had come to stay and this gave me a problem. Usually I don't like strangers in the house and I hide but when I saw how much stuff she'd brought and put in the little bedroom downstairs I realised she could be here for a long time. I couldn't hide for more than a few hours or I got hungry. I decided to see how easy it would be to avoid her and if Mum still remembered to feed me. I must say that Granny was very nice. She brought me presents and said my name really nicely … 'Kimmy Cat', she called me. I liked that. It made me feel special.

One evening they were watching that funny box with pictures and I was looking at them from up the stairs. I didn't want to join them as Granny was sitting on my chair. She saw me and called me down. I wasn't sure but after thinking for a good long time I decided to go and say, 'Hello'. Mum looked dead pleased as I usually ran into a cupboard. I liked having Granny here now as it turned out that I got extra food because Mum was feeling guilty and Granny (or Auntie Granny as she said she preferred. It's funny how humans like to be called 'auntie' when they get to know you.) fed me because she wanted to make me like her. So I got double portions. That was good. That was very good. I was quite sad when she packed up her things and Mum said goodbye to her. Had she left already? One of the people who loved me wasn't here any more.

Top Tip

When there are visitors to the house take time to check them out before honouring them with a purr or any reaction at all. If they really want you to like them they will try hard and this can be enormous fun. If they haven't brought you a present, don't even think of sitting on their knee.

Thursday 25th October

I thought that Mum was missing Auntie Granny because she kept herself very busy all of a sudden. She went out and came back carrying lots of heavy bags and went out to the courtyard. She didn't really go out there very often because the weather wasn't often good but I sat and watched as she dug tiny holes and pressed little fat round things into the earth. Then she covered them with stuff from a bag.

She saw me watching and told me, 'You wait Kimmy. These will come up in the spring and we'll get lots of lovely colourful flowers.'

I wasn't so sure but it was good to see Mum being so active and cheerful.

'I can't wait to see how these turn out Kimmy,' she said.

I wondered how anything good could come out of those tiny little balls. I watched until I became bored and went inside for my nap.

Chapter Eighteen

Clocks

Sunday 28th October

Something funny happened today. Mum slept for longer and I got my breakfast really late although it was the same time. Funny that? It was also a lot darker when I went out into the courtyard. Strange …

I was sure that Mum's clock wasn't right. Just when it was getting dark was when my tummy told me it was time to eat but for some reason I was told to wait. And in the mornings when I woke up and went to get my breakfast in the pop up box - it hadn't popped up! What was wrong?

Monday 29th October

Mum went to see a family who are after two very posh sounding dogs and she was pleased because they lived just around the corner. She could be quite lazy sometimes and didn't always like to exert herself too much. I heard her moaning on the phone because the woman has four kids that were taught at home.

'It'll be bedlam,' she said, 'and I bet the kids are dead spoilt'.

Well it turned out that the family was the nicest Mum had met yet (next to another family she had really liked who took two kittens) and although their home was in the centre of Bath, it had a lovely big garden hidden at the back. The children were charming and she fell in love with them all.

'Those dogs are going to be *so* lucky,' said Mum on the phone before adding, 'I knew this would work out'.

What a lie! Mum should admit that she often pre-judged people and then was pleasantly surprised.

But the day held one more unpleasant surprise for me. Mum had decided to take me to the vet to get my nails shortened as she says I had been ripping up the furniture too much and getting them caught. I have no idea why this was so important but had to admit that they were very long ….I just didn't want to go to the vet's as something horrible always happens to me when I go there.

When Mum pulled out the carrying box and carried towards it I made the most dreadful fuss. I made my body go all big and heavy and wriggled around as much as I could. I tried to grab the side of the sofa with one paw and a lamp stand with the other. I used all my soon to be less sharp claws to attack and even when I heard Mum cry out that I had, 'drawn blood', I didn't stop. *I was not going to go in that box!*

Mum was stronger than me - just. And she got me in and shut the lid before I could try another escape tactic. I let out a long cry instead.

I let my body go dead in the box so I would be as heavy as possible to carry and I screamed and wailed the whole way. But we got to the now familiar surgery where I hoped Mum would be told off for being 'too anxious'. But no such luck.

When my name was called I was carried in and once again I was gently tipped out onto the counter. I glowered at the vet and wondered what he would do if I lashed him with my sharp claws? Then I remembered he had the injections and decided to stay calm instead.

I heard Mum telling him that my nails were too long and that I kept pulling up the carpet. He lifted my paw and agreed that was so and with two sets of firm arms around me I felt him snip at each paw until my claws were short again.

'Is that all?' He asked and I hoped Mum would say, 'Yes', but perhaps mindful of the fact that she was paying for this she said, 'Would you mind popping Kimmy on the scales?'

'Meeeeeeee?'

I can barely bring myself to write this part of the story but to my shame and horror, the scales were outside the small private room. They were in the big room where all the people and their cats and dogs sat. Everyone could see as first my box was weighed and then me in my box. I sloped down with embarrassment.

'Five and a half kilos,' shouted the vet so that everyone could hear. I think people out on the pavement probably heard and it seemed to me that each one of those people were all staring at me and laughing.

One woman hung her head and I could hear a loud snigger. She pressed a glove into her mouth.

Another sighed and said,. 'That's pretty fat'.

A third said, 'Oh, it's not *that* bad'.

And a fourth said, 'I thought that box looked heavy'.

I was carried back into the room and the vet added something to my medical records that he kept for each visit. He had them on a screen like the one that Mum did her writing on. I hoped he wasn't writing *'Fat'*.

'How bad is that?' said Mum and I wanted to scream, 'Not bad at all!'

'She is about a pound overweight'.

'Oh that's okay,' sighed Mum sucking in her stomach.

'No. A pound for a cat who should be four - four and a half kilos is more like a stone for us. She really needs to lose weight. How much does she eat?'

'Er, a small breakfast at 5 am, then another at 8, a light lunch and then supper and something before she goes to bed'.

'That's far too much!'

Mum doesn't often go silent but she didn't speak for a few moments but when she did she appeared to put up a fight.

'But she is always hungry and asking for food. What can I do? Just let her starve?

'Yes. Would you give a fat person a Mars Bar?'

Again, Mum said nothing.

The Vet produced a big bag of food and said, 'Try this. It is dry and will be better for her. This should help get the weight off. Just two small meals a day.'

Had I heard correctly? How could I exist on two *small* meals a day? Was he mad? Or more to the point was Mum?

But she carried me out and paid £37 to the nurse who nodded sympathetically.

'My cat was fat too,' she said.

I am NOT fat.

I wished Mum had pointed out that with the clocks not working I am not getting fed on time so am hungrier than usual. If she just put her clocks right I wouldn't have to suffer this terrible humiliation. But it only got worse.

Chapter Nineteen

The Diet

Tuesday 6th November

When we got back from the vet's yesterday it was teatime and I was starving. I looked up as appealingly as I possibly could at Mum and waited for her to go to the cupboard and get me one of my little packets out. Maybe she would go to the fridge and get me chicken – or a tin of tuna perhaps?

But instead she opened that huge bag that the vet sold her and shook out some of the contents onto a very tiny saucer. It was so tiny that some of the stuff fell off the side and she had to scoop it up and return it to the packet. She picked me up and put me on the window seat where I now like to be fed and I looked at the plate with horror. What was this? It was totally inedible. Dry, tasteless, colourless. And there was hardly any of it. This was not fair. I wanted my nice dinner and I wanted it *now*.

I began to cry pathetically but Mum just walked away saying something like, 'This is for your own good Kimmy'.

My own good? How could that be?

I barely slept because I was so hungry and at dawn I managed to just about stumble down the stairs to the kitchen to find my pop up breakfast. But the feeder was empty and was lying open. She hadn't put anything in it! No breakfast.

I climbed back up the stairs and into the bedroom and despite the late stages of starvation managed to jump on the bed to wake Mum. She groaned and pushed me away but I persisted. 'Kimmy, you're on a diet,' she kept moaning and finally I had to admit defeat. She wasn't going to get up and feed me. Not unless I tried something else. I hooked my paw into the shutter and pushed and then pulled but when it opened just darkness came into the room. That wasn't going to wake anyone up. I tried to go back to sleep but ended up pacing first the room and then Mum's bed. At last, she stumbled out of bed and down the stairs and this time she gave me something to eat from my usual packets. But the portion was tiny.

'You can have a little more later,' she said as I gulped the food down. In a very few seconds it had all gone leaving just a very empty saucer behind.

'You heard the vet. I have to give you about half what you were getting before,' but she was yawning and then went back upstairs to bed leaving a very hungry cat in the kitchen.

The day didn't get any better either. Later on I had the other half of the packet I usually get all of and that evening I got that yucky dried stuff. By bedtime I was like a skinny rake. I was a shadow of my former self. Surely this dieting lark was now over?

Wednesday 7th November

I sat watching Mum stuff herself with delicious looking food and watched her so intently that she finally put down what she was eating and sighed.

I was still on a diet but to be fair Mum now says that until I am at my target weight she is going to diet too. I didn't like to say ….She said that since she had to stop going to her running club when she hurt her ankle, she had been piling on the pounds. So, if I have to starve then so should she.

She said that from now on she would only eat when I did and would eat less too. We were two girls dieting together doing the 'Kimmy Diet'. I felt a bit better now. Just a bit.

Friday 9th November

Mum went off in the morning saying she was going to that London place where she used to live. I knew she had been feeling a bit homesick for it but I can't think why, she had me and this beautiful house. What more could a person want?

She had left quite early and was gone a long time and it was dark when she got back carrying lots of bags, a London newspaper and looking both white and grey at the same time. She looked as if someone had thrown a bag of soot over her but her face was very pale like she'd had all her blood drained out of her.

I met her at the door and ran into the kitchen with her close behind me.

'Oh Kimmy! It was dreadful. So crowded and loud and everyone was rude there!' she said as she spooned food onto my plate. I gave a little mew that she thought was a reply but was really a hint that she was taking too long with the food.

Now mash it, I thought as she was still talking and my food looked decidedly lumpy.

She stabbed at it with a fork and got it all the way I liked it. Tiny bite sized pieces. She put it down on the floor for me, then saw I was on the window ledge and picked it up and put it there instead.

'So … I was so pleased I lived here in Bath and that we won't be moving back to London'.

I gulped and nearly choked but composed myself quickly. Mum had been thinking of moving back to London? She must have been feeling more homesick than I thought. But when she said 'we' did she mean 'I'?

Top Tip

If your Mum has been out make sure you are waiting at the door looking as hungry and pathetic as possible. She will feel so guilty at leaving you that she will feed you straight away even if it is not a meal-time. If your Mum goes out to work this also applies but cry piteously when she comes in so that feeding you is the first thing she does.

Monday 12th November

I had been doing so well on my diet that Mum had brought me back a packet of chicken slices to eat. She said they were very low calorie but despite this I loved them and more or less decided that I wouldn't eat anything else in future. She put my little (very little) dish down for me and I ate it so fast that I barely tasted what was on the plate. Then I chased the empty saucer all around the floor trying to extract every last bit of flavour. I think Mum got the message and gave me a little more. Delicious!

I think winter is a stupid time to diet because it is so cold outside and anyone could see that I am not really fat - it is just that I have my thicker winter coat.

Thursday 15th November

Auntie Granny phoned and told Mum that her cat Jamie had mistaken the letterbox for a cat-flap and he had tried to squeeze through it. I heard them both laughing about it for ages. Well, if I get any thinner I will be able to do the same. But it made me proud to know that I am not as stupid as that. I must admit I am starting to like my new slim body. Not that I didn't like the old one!

(Note from Kimmy's Mum; Kimmy had been eating two to three packets of Whiskas a day plus she had a plate of dried food down at all times. She was starting to eat more and more and wasn't exercising much. The vet wanted her to have two meals a day with at least one of them being this low calorie dried Prescription Science Diet. I think he'd have liked both meals to be the Science Diet but she didn't like it much. With an alarming rise in pet obesity I was keen that Kimmy not be part of that. I hadn't had her long and I want to keep her for longer. It is stupid to let your pet get fat as it is so hard to help them lose the weight. So take action now! It will be worth it in the end!)

Monday 19th November

Mum got on her bicycle which she keeps locked to the railing outside.

She said she was going to a part of Bath she hadn't been to before. Somewhere less posh and old, I think. When she got back she told me she had found a pet shop selling some new food for me! I felt very excited. What cat doesn't want to hear that new food was in the offing? I was even more pleased to hear that this food not only had to be *specially* ordered but was being *delivered* by a man in a van as well. This was beyond all my expectations and was something I could only aspire to as a very spoiled cat. I couldn't help but think of Ginger (who I haven't thought about for ages). He probably got own-brand food that his Mum has wheeled home in the supermarket trolley. Later that same trolley probably ended up in the canal. Oh, the bliss of being truly pampered.

Tuesday 20th November

The man with the food arrived. Mum was cross because she had to wait in all afternoon even though the man was very nice when he arrived.

'Kimmy, your new food is here!' she shouted up the stairs to where I was relaxing by the radiator.

Later she scraped it onto a tiny saucer for me to eat and do you know what? It was yucky. Completely disgusting. Low calorie food stinks. It has no taste at all and I spat it out.

Top Tip

If your Mum tries to give you anything 'Low Calorie' just refuse to eat it or put your paw down your throat and throw it up. For those of you who can't read or don't know what 'low calorie' is then look at the label and look for this word, 'Lite'. Don't eat it.

I've been told that Christmas is on the way and that I was to play some part in it. For some reason Mum thought I should not only send cards but she also thought that my photo should be used for them. She decided to use the photographs she took for the Bath Cats and Dogs Home Photographic Competition. It was of me lying on my back with the sun pouring through the window. I looked very happy and relaxed in that picture. She said she would make a card and then tell people that it was the winning photograph but I just yawned as it was time for my nap.

It was certainly cold enough to think of Christmas and Mum said that the animals at the Home must be very cold in their runs and cages. Unlike me they don't have cosy fires to lie beside or comfy beds to snuggle on. They had just launched their Winter Appeal. This was when they asked the Public to give them food and blankets. I lay on our warm bed that was still toastie warm from the electric blanket and the central heating had just clicked on. I looked at Mum and wondered what we could do to help. I hoped that she wasn't thinking of bringing another cat home? I couldn't imagine life as anything but an 'only cat'. Mum sprang out of bed and I followed her down the stairs for my breakfast.

'Just think of those poor cats,' said Mum who was determined not to give up on this one as she looked at the frosty windows.

I was too interested in my food but had to admit that I was glad I was here and not there. I would have a nice full tummy in a moment and then I would have a nap somewhere very comfortable and cosy.

The next thing Mum was going through my food cupboard and pulling things out on to the floor in an untidy heap.

'You don't need all this,' she said but I begged to differ. I noticed that the low calorie food hadn't joined the collection but had been returned to the cupboard. Then she went downstairs and I could hear her rummaging around. She came back up triumphant having found my old igloo bed. It was like a big bubble but all warm and padded with woolly material. I hadn't used it once as I didn't like it.

I gave a mew of objection.

'Kimmy you never use it! And it's too small for you!' Well, that was true. I had never even been in it. Mum stuffed it into a bag and then I heard the front door slam. She had left to take *my* things up to the Home for the cats.

I wished she had taken that stupid tent.

I finished my breakfast and went upstairs to pop under the duvet again. In a few moments I was asleep. Zzzzzzzzzzzz.

Wednesday 21st November

I was so hungry that I could barely walk but I managed to get up on my hind legs and look out the window of the front of the house where I am not allowed to even look. This is because that's where all the cars were. I was curious to see this world that I was excluded from. Mum watched me and laughed before telling me off.

'Kimmy! Get down!'

I got down and went back upstairs again. The outside world didn't look too interesting to me.

Mum said that today it was raining cats and dogs but I didn't see either, I just saw loads of wet stuff coming from the sky. It was also cold and very dark so I was glad that I could just go and take a nice long nap while Mum struggled into a plasticey coat.

'I'm giving blood today, Kimmy,' she told me and I wondered what that meant. I had seen the red sticky stuff on Mum's arm when I was play fighting with her and I'd forgotten to keep my claws in. It is excellent fighting practice for us cats for when we might come across a rat or a mouse. But Mum had always screamed with pain. Was she going to go and actually *give* this blood? Would dozens of fierce cats be scratching her? I wouldn't want to hear her shouting!

She opened the door that I am not allowed to even sit near and went off slamming it loudly behind her. But not before I had been showered with wind and cold rain.

Later she came back all wet and wearing a big bandage on her arm.

'I have to take it easy for the rest of the day,' she told me but I knew Mum didn't need much excuse for that.

When she was in her big bath laying in the soapy water (funny that, humans hate getting wet outside but they love it inside?) I don't often go into the bathroom because the door is often shut and because being a cat I don't like water. But today I was worried that with relaxing and taking a bath at this different time, Mum would forget that she hadn't fed me yet. It had to be supper time? I hadn't had a meal for ages. I walked round the room mewing pathetically.

'Kimmy! It is only three o'clock!' said Mum as if that meant something to me. I just knew I was hungry and when a cat has to remind her carer to feed her it is pretty sad.

Later as I ate my supper, Mum said, 'I wonder if the vet from the Telegraph could give me some tips on how to keep you happy while you're dieting?' I knew Mum liked reading the big newspaper on a Saturday even though it had so many pages. She would read aloud from the pet problem page and try and get me to show some interest.

I'd forgotten I was dieting! That's why I was so hungry!

I heard Mum tapping away on her laptop. She liked to write to newspapers and things because she is a writer and she says that is sometimes the only way to see her name in print.

'And send!' exclaimed Mum hitting a key on her laptop. And then she picked me up. 'I have written to Pete Wedderburn, the Telegraph's vet to ask if he can give me some diet tips for you.' Mum used to read Celia Haddon's page but she had left now.

Hmmmm. As long as it involves a lot more food, then I was happy.

Friday 23rd November

Mum got a reply from Pete Wedderburn at the Telegraph.

Thank you for your query which I may not be able to print in the paper due to space restrictions - (*trust Mum to be long-winded*) but I think that she is just a hungry cat, and she has learned to eat at 5 am. For your sleep's sake, I would continue to give her a small meal at that time with the automatic feeder, (*happy days*) **but I also think that you should ask your vet about special weight loss diets - these have added bulk but less calories, so she can eat enough to feel full without ingesting too many calories. Also make sure she gets plenty of play and other activities during the day. Good Luck!**

So, he wasn't able to print her letter. It would have been good to be featured in a National *posh* newspaper. That had to be posher than the Bath Chronicle otherwise known as *The Chronic*. Maybe they'd have used my picture? I always enjoyed lying on the pages of the big papers. The bigger and thicker the paper the better it is. Mum was frowning with disappointment. But then when he said that I was obviously a 'very hungry cat' – yes, that is true! He suggested that Mum go back to filling my pop up timer box with early breakfast so she could sleep later. That was very good news …! But he also suggested that she give me that low fat rubbish that I hate so much. Still, I am getting my early breakfast back!

He wished Mum 'good luck'. Why? She had me.

Chapter Twenty

Christmas is Coming!

Saturday 24th November

We got our first Christmas card! I say *we* because it had my name on it too including the envelope. Mum seemed dead chuffed although she said something about, 'It's only November'. She spent the rest of the day writing her cards. She had one that she made herself. She used a photo of me to insert into a card and I had to admit I did look gorgeous. But then I am a beautiful cat.

I was in a good mood because I had had an early breakfast and then had come up to wake Mum and say thank you for such a treat. Unfortunately I think I must have run a bit fast as when I got upstairs I felt a bit sick. I sat retching by the bed for ages until Mum woke up and put a newspaper underneath me.

Charming. I was nearly being sick and she just went back to sleep!

I always knew when Mum was going out because she took a long bath and then got all dressed up first. Tonight she dressed in a fancy skirt with a new top I hadn't seen before. There are lots of things in her wardrobe I haven't seen. It is funny how many clothes she has yet she nearly always wears the same things. She still didn't know many people in Bath yet and these were new friends who had asked her round for dinner - Barrington and Marion or 'Baz' and 'Maz' as Mum called them. I had to admit that she looked very nice but I really didn't want her to go out. I wanted her to stay at home with me. If she went out I'd be lonely so I looked up at her as appealingly as I could. She lay down on the bed beside me and began to brush me gently.

'I think you look slimmer already Kimmy'. I knew she was being kind and she certainly looked very glam but I was ashamed to say I was so upset at her leaving me that I swiped her fiercely with my paw. She screamed and then I swiped again and again. Each time I dug in my claws until Mum's arm was running blood. She gave a startled cry and jumped off the bed. I lashed my tail back and forth but seeing that Mum was angry I also decided to do a bit of a runner. I jumped down under the bed and hid.

I could see her holding her arm under a tap in the bathroom next to the bedroom. I could hear the water running. Then she came back into the bedroom and I watched her inspecting her arm more closely. It had raised white lumps and was swollen. The bleeding had stopped though. I felt bad and wished I hadn't hurt her. I would make it up to her later but right now I was still feeling angry.

'I can't go out like this,' she kept saying.

Mum changed her top from the new one she had planned to wear into something with longer sleeves that would hide the scratches. Then she had to change her skirt as the fresh top didn't look right any more. Then the shoes didn't match. Several changes later she found something she was happy to wear. There was an enormous pile of clothes on the bedroom floor.

‘I’ll have to take anti-histamine now Kimmy, as this is all raised and bumpy,’ said Mum hanging over the side of the bed, looking down at me and holding up her arm. It *did* look raised and bumpy … with funny white lumps.

I didn’t manage to stop her going out though and a few minutes later I heard the door slam behind her as she left. I settled myself down for a long, lonely evening. I wished I hadn’t slashed her just as badly as I had …

She didn’t come back till very, very late but told me she could have stayed longer.

‘It was still in full swing,’ she said as she pulled off the nice clothes. I had no idea what ‘full swing’ was but I noticed that she was all wobbly. ‘But those anti-histamine tablets made me very sleepy and I could hardly keep my eyes open. The wine just made it worse.’

I jumped up beside her and snuggled up, purring my appreciation and by way of an apology. She stroked my ear and made me feel a lot better. A few moments later and we were both sound asleep.

Top Tip

If you want to stop your Mum from going out don’t scratch her too hard or she may have to call an ambulance and then you’ll be in trouble. Try pretending to be very sick instead.

Monday 26th November

Mum was using her litter tray downstairs in my bathroom when I wanted to go to the loo. I usually prefer to be alone. But we were both so comfortable together that we used our trays at the same time. I was bursting and couldn't wait. Mum looked surprised when she saw me walk in and get into my litter box but I thought, 'We're both girls together'.

Bathroom duties done, we then had breakfast. Coffee and toast for Mum and a small plate of Felix in gravy for me - it's my new favourite. I went off Whiskas just after Mum came home with three big boxes of it. She said it was 'on offer' and I hated eating food that was cheap.

Mum went out and when she came back *hours* later I noticed that she was limping again. She said she had gone to Bristol to show someone my 'Kimmy Diaries'. She came back very upset saying, 'It was a wild goose chase. I had to walk all over the place and my leg is sore.' I am not sure why she would chase wild geese but today she seemed to be in such a lot of pain that she told me she was going to the doctor just as soon as she'd been to the dentist. The doctor and the dentist in one afternoon? That's like a double vet's appointment, isn't it? But then a thought struck me. Was my Mum getting old? Or did her sore leg have anything to do with the running club she had just gone back to?

Mum seemed very upset. She was planning to run the Bath Half Marathon next year in aid of Bath Cats and Dogs Home. I am not sure what a half marathon is but I know that it is half as far as something very, very far. So that still makes it a long way. The idea is that she would run and people gave her money to do it – I think. But with her ankle being so sore this may mean she can't.

'Oh Kimmy. Have I made a mistake moving to Bath? I've not had much luck since I've been here'.

Oh no. Was Mum thinking of going back to London? Would I like it there? And what if she wasn't able to take me? Isn't that what had happened to my last home? She had moved and not taken me with her. Was the same thing about to happen to me again? Auntie Jan from the Home phoned to tell Mum that her pictures of me hadn't won the photographic competition. I could hear Mum sighing deeply. I think she was more upset than me. I knew I was gorgeous. I don't need a prize – although it would have been good to have had my portrait painted. But Mum is quite upset. Still, at least I was entered. Auntie Jan wasn't allowed to enter her Mickey (my *boyfriend*) because she works there.

I think Mum should have used a professional photographer. I don't think she really knew what she was doing. She even took it in black and white. Maybe she has never heard of colour? Why didn't she ask Auntie Jan to take it?

Saturday 1st December

Mum was supposed to be going to her friend Debbie's birthday party but she can't because her ankles are too sore - they are both swollen now. I was sorry that she was in pain but am glad that she wasn't leaving me or going to that London place because if she enjoyed herself she might regret leaving it in the first place. I know she has been feeling a bit homesick - like I felt when I was first left at Bath Cats and Dogs Home. But I had no choice but to get on with my new life and maybe Mum should do the same. I was so scared that she'd move back to London and leave me behind and the more I thought of it, the more worried I got.

The one good thing is that with all this worry - Mum had forgotten about me being on a diet and gave me something to eat almost every time I asked. Or maybe she doesn't care about me any more because she knew she was giving me back to the Home and was feeding me up?

Auntie Jan phoned. Mum had sent her the first few chapters of 'The Kimmy Diaries' to read and Jan thought they were funny! The two of them sat giggling on the phone for ages while I listened. I hope Mum meant for them to be funny because the way Jan was laughing - I could hear it down the phone - they'd have to be pretty bad to have had that effect. What is so funny about my life? I went back to sleep.

Tuesday 4th December

Mum has cheered up enough to put up a Christmas tree in the room she called the drawing room. It had big wide branches and she covered it in all sorts of colourful balls and bows and funny little lights so it looked really pretty when it was lit up. I was pleased to see Mum looking happier and hoped that she stayed that way. I wondered if I could climb the tree. It was ages since I'd done that. I wasn't sure I could remember how to do it.

Mum started to wrap some of her presents to put under the tree and I spotted a bit of brightly coloured paper that she wasn't using. I went and sat on it and began to purr. 'Oh Kimmy, you look lovely sitting there,' said Mum and she stroked me. I hoped she would let me have this bit of paper for life and not just for Christmas.

Mum's good mood changed when she went out into the courtyard and found out that I have been digging up all those funny little round things she has been planting under the soil. She had covered the big pots with a sort of net but being Kimmy, I managed to pull that off to do my 'business' and while I was digging I thought, 'Hello, what are these?'

'You've dug up my bulbs Kimmy!' exclaimed Mum, 'And I can't even re-plant them as the soil is too hard. Anyway, it looks as if you have eaten some of them'.

I tried to look as innocent as possible. After all, how was I to know?

But one thing's for sure – whatever comes up in the spring will certainly be a surprise.

Chapter Twenty-One

Home

Friday 7th December

Mum brought a new friend round to the house. They both had hair the same colour but this lady dressed very smartly - as if she was going to work in an office. They had met when Mum went to her house for a home visit because she wanted to have a kitten. They quickly discovered that they both came from the same part of London and had recently moved to Bath. The new friend was called Annie and she had now adopted a cat from the Home too - although she got a bigger cat as she was too close to a main road. I didn't know the cat as we weren't there at the same time. Mum said it was spooky how much they had in common but I still don't like it when strangers come to the house so I hissed at her and arched my back when I saw her on the stairs.

'Kimmy!' exclaimed Mum.

It didn't stop them going out and after they had left I worried that they would talk about their old part of London and then Mum would feel homesick again and want to move back there. Maybe I shouldn't have hissed at Annie. It was hard to work out if it would help or not. Now Mum would feel easier about leaving me behind if I am nasty.

I decided that as from tomorrow I would be a nicer cat. So when Mum came back much later and all-wobbly, I purred and rubbed around her ankles. I let her see how gorgeous I could be. She'd never want to leave me now.

Saturday 8th December

It was raining very badly when we woke up. The wind had been so bad during the night and I had hardly slept because I thought the rain might come through the roof. I could hear it lashing against the windows and the shutters and window panes rattled. Mum looked worried when she turned on the radio.

Someone sounding very serious was saying that a big storm was happening and that it might flood again like it did in the summer. He was telling people to stay indoors and *not go out.*

'I have to go out Kimmy, but I will leave you lots of food and I'll be back later'.

I knew where she was going and I wished that maybe with the wind and rain she would stay with me. She must want to go very much to leave on a day like this.

Mum was taking the train back to where she used to live. Not the same place exactly but somewhere very close - Twickenham. She was meeting an old friend and would be looking at the places that she said she was missing. These were places that maybe she had talked to Annie about last night. She said she hadn't dared go back in case it made her homesick but now on the rainiest day of a very wet year, she was pulling on an ugly coat with a hood and setting off. I, Kimmy, was left behind with just a dish of dried food and my pop up feeder set to go off at supper time.

I settled myself down for a long anxious wait until she came home. Soon I was asleep. Then I woke up and went back to sleep again. I wandered round the house, ate some dried food and had another nap. But between naps I was worrying. Was Mum going to leave me and go back to London? Or maybe she wouldn't come back at all? I wondered what would happen if she just stayed. How would I manage on my own? At least I knew where my food was kept.

The rain lasted all day and it turned from gloomy to dark and still no sign of Mum. I heard the post thudding through the letterbox and landing on a soggy heap on the mat. There was no fire on to warm me and the TV box, that she liked to watch, remained off. The house was very, very quiet. I had eaten my supper from the pop up feeder with no one to watch me and was just tucking my paws under me as I settled down for another nap when I heard her rattling at the door. At least I hoped it was her. As she came through the doorway a big whoosh of cold and icy water flew in with her.

I did that thing I knew she really loved. I ran down the stairs to where it bends round the corner and I put my little head around so she could just see my face peering down. I blinked because I was still sleepy. She loved this and it always made her smile and then she told me how lovely I was. I had a feeling that tonight I had to use all the tricks of a very clever cat to really make her love me.

'Oh Kimmy!' she said as she pulled off the horrible wet coat and flung it on the floor. I noticed that her umbrella was now all floppy and lay uselessly beside the coat. Her hair was wet and stuck to the top of her face. 'Am I glad to see you!'

I ran down the stairs and as a treat I let her pick me up. I melted in her arms and began to purr. I didn't stop her when she began to prepare a second supper for me. This time, it was my favourite chicken slices from the fridge. She was talking very fast.

'It was so *wet* and the train was crowded. It took forever. The pub didn't look at all like I remembered it and they didn't even have all their Christmas decorations up or the fire burning. (Mum had told me that the pub was always lit up with tiny little fairy lights and in winter had a fire burning in the grate). The wine was just okay my friend was late and wouldn't stop talking. So I couldn't get a word in having come so far. The play wasn't at all funny. I could barely see the river for mist and I just wanted to get home - to you'.

I purred my approval. This sounded bad - or rather it sounded good for me. She had not enjoyed herself. But Mum hadn't finished.

'At the station they were doing engineering work so they stopped the trains but they didn't tell anyone what to do. It was only by chance I found out … and I only got as far as Swindon on the way back. It was full of rowdy football fans. I had to get *two* buses and a cab home.'

I didn't really know what Mum was going on about exactly but I knew she'd had a bad day and was glad to be home. To *this* home. *Where she lived with me.*

Mum looked very tired as she poured a glass of that red stuff that seemed to make her feel better. She sank down onto the sofa and slumped forward.

‘I am never going to London again Kimmy. It was horrible and I had forgotten how gloomy it can look on a day like this. I’d never seen it look that bad before’.

I pressed myself up against her and then jumped onto her lap. I felt her hands smoothing my fur and it was very soothing and relaxing. I began to purr.

‘I really missed you Kimmy. It is good to be home’. Does that sound like a Mum who is homesick and thinking of leaving her cat to move back to where she used to live? I think not.

Then she went upstairs to take one of those baths that she loved so much.

I couldn’t be happier!

And outside the rain had stopped.

Top Tip

If your Mum (or Dad) has been out all day and comes back looking very tired or upset, make sure you make a big fuss of them. They will be very grateful and you will probably get an extra portion of food out of it - or some extra spoiling at least.

Sunday 9th December

Another cold, windy day and Mum woke up with sore ankles again so we both spent the day together doing absolutely nothing but eating and sleeping. Mum read the papers and I sat on the pages. It was total bliss. I loved having an all-girls day.

Wednesday 12th December

I couldn't believe it when I saw Mum standing on a chair hanging these glass things on a long wire from the tree in the courtyard. What was she doing? Is she trying to make the tree outside look like the tree inside? I had to tell her it wouldn't work as they looked very different. One is tall and bushy and the other is just branches stretched against the wall. It used to have more branches and green leaves but some men came along and cut them off. It made the courtyard look far bigger and Mum said they'd grow back. But until now the tree had looked rather bare.

When it got dark I found out what she had been doing. She pressed a little switch in the basement and the lights came on outside! It looked very pretty but I was glad to watch them from inside because it was very cold. Brrrrrrrrrrrrrr.

Friday 14th December

Mum had been doing so much shopping that she told me she had loads of points on the card she used at one particular store. I had no idea what that meant but she also said that if she bought a camera she would get even more of these points and then she would be able to buy something else. How could buying lots of things help you to buy *more* things? It all sounded a bit complicated but she went out and came back with a new camera a bit like the one that Auntie Jan at the Home had only a lot cheaper. It took pictures that you could see instantly. She says that I could use them in my 'autocatography' and she kept going round taking pictures of me. I woke up and she was taking a photo and I went to sleep with her taking my photo. She made me sit under the Christmas tree …. Click! And I rolled on my back … Click! I sat on my bit of paper …. Click! I liked all this attention but wished she had bought it sooner and then maybe I would have won the competition up at the Home. I think that is why she bought it. I hope she asks Auntie Jan to help show her how to use it …

Mum's found this great club for me. It is on the in-ter-net and is called www.unitedcats.com, United Cats. It is a special place where cats can meet other cats in cyberspace - wherever that is. Soon I had hundreds of friends including Mickey, Porsche and Cassie - who live just up the road so I didn't have to go all the way to cyberspace to meet them. But I also became friends with Ronaldinho, Mew Mew and his little 'sister' Pig, Mugger, Kittibits, Cisco and Pancho, Betsey … and too many to mention. But needless to say it is far funnier for my Mum and Auntie Jan than it is for me although I like being popular and getting 'catmail'. But I have to admit I am proud to be on cyberspace now, I'm just not so keen when she tries to dress me up and take photographs.

Monday 17th December

Something was up. I could tell. Mum was putting clothes into a bag as well as some of the presents from under the tree – including some of the ones I had my eye on. She kept writing notes on bits of paper and giving me lots of extra cuddles - which I hate (unless I was in the mood). She usually cuddled me when something was going on. If I didn't know her better I would say that she was going away? No! Not so close to Christmas. She couldn't leave me alone at Christmas could she?

Tuesday 18th December

Mum had gone away! She took the bag that I'd seen her putting things in yesterday and left soon after breakfast.

'I have to go to the hospital first. To have my ankle x-rayed although it is feeling much better today. Then I'm going to the airport,' she told me as if that would make any sense to me at all. I stared up at her before going to sit on my piece of paper.

I knew for sure that she'd gone because my cat feeder came to feed me later on that afternoon and I was pretty fed up with her. How could Mum have gone away so close to Christmas? Would she be back on time? Would I get any presents? I thought Mum loved me but maybe she didn't if she was leaving me behind. I felt very small and unhappy and after the cat feeder left I went upstairs and had an early night. Maybe tomorrow when I woke up Mum would be back?

Wednesday 19th December

Still no sign of Mum but my pop up box opened at 5 am, so at least I got to force down a decent breakfast. My cat feeder came by later but I ignored her even though I was beginning to like her really. She wasn't my Mum and it was Christmas, I hated being left all alone. The shutters had been closed over the back doors and windows, so I couldn't even go out into the courtyard and the house was all dark downstairs. I spent the day catching up on my sleep, relaxing, cleaning myself, looking at the tree and sitting on my bit of paper. A pretty busy day really.

Thursday 20th December

My cat feeder told me that Mum was coming back today and I was very pleased. She had been gone for months! Christmas would be over if she didn't get back soon. Later on I heard a noisy car pull up outside the house and footsteps getting out. Then I heard the familiar high pitched voice of someone I knew very well ….The front door opened.

'Kimmy the Kim, Kimmy Kim!' Mum is the only one who greeted me like this.

I was on my bit of paper but I left it immediately to come to the top of the stairs to peer down. Mum! And she wasn't alone – Granny was with her. Between them they had loads of luggage but I'm glad to say they made a huge fuss of me and I got to rub round both sets of their ankles.

They made tea and sat at the table and I washed my face. I was glad to see Mum even if she wasn't on her own. I would tolerate Gran if she had come to stay (and as she was carrying bags, she must be) and as I remembered she had been pretty nice to me the last time. Maybe I would get doubly spoiled? I decided not to hide - especially when I saw the extra presents going around the tree.

And it turned out that Mum's ankle *was* better. She'd had it x-rayed and they'd found nothing so she would now be able to take part in the Bath Half Marathon, running for Bath Cats and Dogs Home. She seemed very pleased about that.

Just when I thought that the day was shaping up to be a good one after all, Mum suddenly grabbed me and before I could even think what might be going on I was shoved into that pet carrier again. Not another trip to the vet's!

'Come on Kimmy. It won't take a second and you do need to get your nails trimmed. Before Christmas …'

This time it was colder and an icy blast met us as Mum opened the door and it was much darker. I mewed as pitifully as I could and Gran said something about how bad the traffic was but we eventually got over the road and with each step I was getting closer to that surgery again. I was hardly out of the place!

This time the room was empty when we got inside.

'We're first,' I heard Mum tell Gran. She didn't even need to tell the nurse my details. She knew them already!

'Kimmy, isn't it?' she asked. But just as Mum was nodding a woman came dashing in clutching a cat who wasn't even in a basket. She was holding it in her coat and the cat seemed quite limp. I could see that it was un-groomed as well. Clearly this cat was not very well. The woman holding her looked pale and was very agitated. The nurse took her details and Mum said that she could go in front of us. Yes, they could all go in front of us as far as I was concerned. Maybe we could just go home now? The woman was too distracted to even register what we were saying to her and walked straight in to see the vet. The door was closed behind her. Mum placed my carrier on a bench and she and Gran started to talk to a man who had just come in with two very noisy cats in a big basket. They both seemed to have totally forgotten about me so I gave a little mew to remind them.

After what seemed like a very long time, the woman came out but she didn't have the cat with her any more and her face was wet with crying. We all went silent and I suddenly felt full of fear Oh no! So it was true. Cats could visit the vet and then never come home again.

'She was very sick,' the woman told everyone in the room and they all nodded numbly. It seemed that no one knew what to say. My Gran put her arm around the woman but she just wanted to get out and a moment later she had gone.

We all stared at each other in silence and I desperately wanted them to take me home and not into that dreadful room. The room where the cat had gone in but not come out again.

'Kimmy please,' said a voice. It was the other vet, the lady. The other vet must be off.

I was carried into that room again and I pushed myself into the back of my carrier and decided that I wouldn't come out. Mum was saying something about the cat before me.

'It was for the best,' the vet said. 'Now what can we do for Kimmy?'

'Not the same as she did for the last cat', I thought.

Mum had eased me out of the box and I fell out with a thump. I sensed that even she just wanted to get me home now.

'Her nails need clipping. She keeps scratching the furniture'.

So that was it! If I scratched the furniture I would be taken to the vet! I felt the usual strong arms around me and then I heard the sound of the snipping. Snip, snip, snip. My nails lay on the counter.

'Actually they weren't too bad,' said the vet.

Mum nodded. 'Well, they were done quite recently.' She went to pick me up and pushed me back into the box again and this time I was happy to go back in. But the vet was still speaking.

'We've got some new scales. They're super accurate. They will show if a cat has lost even an ounce. Shall we just pop Kimmy on?'

To be fair Mum hesitated. I think she was regretting bringing me and just wanted to get home.

'No, that's okay thanks,' she said, wrapping her body round me as if to offer some sort of disguise to my wobbly tummy.

'It'll just take a second. It'll be good to know where Kimmy has got to with her little weight problem'.

Weight problem!

I felt myself being lifted and then put into a small tray. Two sets of hands let go of me.

'She's been dieting. We both have,' muttered Mum. 'You know how it is …' her voice trailed off.

'Oh, nearly 6 … no! Not quite. 5.75 kilos. She's put on …!'

There was another deathly hush and then Mum started babbling again.

'I can't believe it. I mean, we've been so careful. Well, maybe over the past few days … with the cold weather … perhaps the cat feeder …?' Mum was rabbiting on.

'You'll need to bring her back for another weigh-in in about six weeks, if that's okay?' asked the vet.

Numbly Mum nodded her head and gathered me up. 'Come on,' she hissed in a whisper.

A moment later we were out on that scary pavement again with all the noise.

'Kimmy's on the 'At risk' register,' said Mum.

'Well I did think she'd put on weight,' said Gran rudely.

They peered in at me and I stared back.

A few minutes later we were warm and dry inside and I was crying for my supper. They surely wouldn't put me on a diet before

Christmas would they? But then I had a more immediate worry. Mum had discovered that I had 'broken into' my timed box by forcing up the lid and now it wouldn't stay down any more.

'Oh Kimmy, you are a greedy cat,' she said. I decided that now was not a good time to demand extra supper.

Friday 21st December

They *had* got me on a diet! Can you believe it? First she went away and left me and now she was starving me again. Not that Mum is a bit good at diets because she had put on weight too! She muttered something about, 'We're both going to lose weight after Christmas,' but it hasn't stopped her giving me portions on tiny little plates while Granny said things like 'Don't give her too much.'

As if …!

And to make matters worse, when they sat down to watch that TV, Granny sat in *my* Chair. It's always been mine and it even has my little blanket on it. **(Note from Kimmy's Mum; I also have a throw on the chair to keep it clean and to stop Kimmy scratching it!)**. I spent the evening staring at Granny until she got very uncomfortable and gave me my seat back. It is very comfy and right by the fire. She sat on another chair - the one I don't use because it is so small.

Saturday 22nd December

Mum had bought me one of those funny calendars where you open a little window each day until Christmas. There was an edible treat in each little hole although I didn't like them much. We'd been opening them for days now and there were only two little doors to go - so it must be Christmas soon. I hoped my presents would be a lot more exciting than these not very nice treats.

Our good mood was broken when Mum had a phone message from her new friend Annie (the one who had the cat) and heard that Annie's new cat had accidentally got out and run away.

'He's lost,' Mum told Gran. They both looked very upset and I felt like crying too as I tried to imagine what it would be like to be 'lost'. No warm fire to sit beside. No regular meals whenever I felt like one. No cosy bed to sleep on or a Mum who did everything for me. I would hate to be lost - especially at Christmas. We all felt very sad for the rest of the day.

Top Tip

If your cat goes missing don't just assume he or she will come home by himself. Try phoning all the local vets to see if she has been brought in (your cat will be micro-chipped). Let the Home know your cat is missing in case anyone brings him in to them. Ask all your neighbours to look out for him and to try all their sheds in case he'd got locked in. Put up posters with a photo of your cat (looking his best) and your phone number so people can ring you if they find him. Call at the back door as often as possible so if you cat is lost he may hear you. Food can be used as an extra incentive! But also try never to let a new cat out for about a month or two so they have time to settle and decide that they want to stay. Of course, I did something quite different when I moved in with Mum (but her courtyard was very secure) but I am Kimmy and not all cats are like me!

Sunday 23rd December

Mum was going to do another one of those home visits. She asked Gran if she'd like to come with her and she said she would. This time Mum was going back to see the nice family with the kids - the ones who took the two posh girl and boy dogs. Mum thought that it would be fun to bring Gran and that they would enjoy it. 'It won't take long,' Mum said but they were gone for ages. When they got back I heard them talking. It turned out that when they'd got round there the posh girl dog wasn't there and Mum had feared the worst until they had sat around the big kitchen table and heard the full story. When they'd got the girl dog home she'd been getting fatter and fatter - but not like me except they thought that at first. They'd even taken her to the vet! But they didn't know what was wrong until one morning they came down and found she'd had lots of little puppies! Because their house wasn't big enough for eight new dogs, they had phoned the Home and been told they could bring her back to a special nursery that they'd made for her. But it all sounded a bit familiar - an unexpected birth at Christmas? And there not being enough room at their house? The boy dog not being the father but being the partner …? It was very seasonal but we all agreed it was a lovely story - a sort of canine nativity. And it would have a happy ending as the Mum dog would come home to her new family when her puppies were bigger and had all found good homes. And being posh dogs they might raise a bit of extra money for Bath Cats and Dog Home. Everyone was happy and loved the story.

I wondered if anyone had asked themselves if I might be pregnant. That would explain a lot.

Mum and Gran were up to something. They'd been shopping and came back with so much food they can't fit it in the fridge or cupboards and they spent the afternoon tidying, re-arranging furniture and putting different looking food out on plates. As the day wore on I began to remember what it was they were doing. They were having a party! I was very upset as I don't like lots of strange people coming to the house so I was quite grateful when Mum picked me up and carried me up to her bedroom. She also brought up my litter tray and some food. Then she went out and closed the door. Well, this wasn't going to be much fun! Closed in the bedroom for Christmas!

Just as I was dropping off for a cosy nap on the bed, I could hear howls of laughter from downstairs and loud high-pitched voices. I think they were all drinking that red stuff that makes Mum wobble about and talk nonsense. I heard Annie's voice (she of the lost cat) and I wondered why she wasn't out looking for him. If it was me lost and out in the cold I would never forgive my Mum if she went to a party and drank wobbly stuff. I would expect her to call the army to help her find me. I began to doze off dreaming of my picture on News at Ten - *'and finally …'*. Then to my horror I could hear footsteps on the stairs - wobbly ones at that. There were three laughing and wobbly people coming into my bedroom. Quickly, I hid myself in Mum's wardrobe amongst her shoes and stuff. They'd never find me there but I was wrong! My hiding place filled with light as the double doors were flung open and a decidedly lopsided Mum stood in front of me.

'There she is,' she said unnecessarily. I made myself even smaller and really stooped low. Behind Mum was my Auntie Jan, from the Home and also Sue who works there too. They all smelt funny. Sort of fruity. And they were all laughing for no real reason.

'I've brought you presents,' said Auntie Jan as Mum picked me from the safety of my hiding place and held me up for all to see. I squirmed in her arms but wondered what she'd bought me. I was covered in sticky red kisses and then hugged some more before they returned me to the safety of the cupboard and they wobbled back down again. Hours and *hours* later, **(note from Kimmy's Mum; it was *two* hours later)**. I heard the door slam and they finally all went home. Mum came up and opened the bedroom door to let me come downstairs again. The kitchen was a terrible mess so I asked to go out the back door into the courtyard and then I hoped that I'd get some more supper. I'd been too stressed to enjoy the earlier one although I had managed to force it down. On my way back upstairs I walked past the Christmas tree and saw that there were a lot of extra presents round it for me!! I was going to have lots to open on Christmas Day, whenever that was! As

Mum and I fell asleep she said, 'Kimmy, we've got friends now and they bring us lovely presents.' I purred my approval and then fell asleep.

Monday 24th December

Mum and Granny both had sore heads and were very quiet. They got up late for breakfast and I was cross with them as I hated it when I had to eat late. They said something about not going anywhere near the shops but a few hours later they pulled on coats and were off out banging the door behind them.

'We're just off to find you another present,' were Mum's last words. *Another* present? That sounded good. But hadn't they left it a bit late?

It seemed like a long, long time before they came back carrying lots of bags and looking tired. I didn't know what was in the bags but hoped there was food for me.

Mum gave me my supper and as I ate it I heard Gran say, 'Kimmy's got a big chest, hasn't she? She's a full double D'.

I have no idea what she was talking about but it sounded rude. I stared at her in silence.

Later, they got dressed up again and said they were going off to Baz and Maz's again (those are the people who came to their party the night before). I would have tried to stop Mum in much the way I had before but didn't like to in front of Granny so I decided I would just have a good nap instead and keep up my strength for Christmas Day. I sat on my piece of Christmas paper, which was by now pieces because I had been playing with it so much, and looked at the lights on the tree. It all looked very pretty and I couldn't wait to see what people have bought me all wrapped up in such lovely paper. Would I get to sit on the paper after, I wondered? I had to admit that these last months have been very good and I was pretty close to being the most spoiled cat in Bath.

Mum and my Gran came back much later. They said they'd had a good time but were now tired and all ready for Christmas. So it was bedtime and I got to curl up on Mum's bed and go into a deep, deep sleep - dreaming of the next day.

Tuesday 25th December

I woke *really* early and was glad to find that Mum hadn't forgotten to fill my pop up box (she'd fixed it, sort of - it still didn't quite close) with breakfast but I was sad to discover it was that nasty dried stuff that I hate. What was she thinking? I spat it out and padded back upstairs and jumped on the bed and paced up and down a few times before patting Mum on her face and licking the hand that peeped out from the duvet. I don't speak much human but what I can say is very clear to anyone who knows cats and I was saying, 'Wake up and feed me now'.

Mum moaned and rolled over so I jumped on top of her and balanced on her hip so that when she rolled over again I fell off with a cry. This woke Mum.

'Kimmy, it's not 7 o'clock yet,' she moaned.

Time meant nothing to me. I persisted in my goal to get Mum to wake up and get my breakfast. I began to mew piteously and was about to resort to pulling up carpet when she murmured, 'Happy Christmas Kimmy!' That was better! She rolled slowly out of bed and began to slowly (very slowly) make her way down the stairs. I wished she would go faster but she was still rubbing her eyes and yawning. When we got downstairs, she began opening the door of 'Kimmy's cupboard' (where my food was) and then went to the fridge instead and took out some of my favourite food - sliced chicken. She cut it up and put it on a tiny dish and I tucked in hungrily.

'Is it time to get up?' We heard a sleepy voice from downstairs.

'No - it's still early,' yawned Mum pulling out some of that coffee stuff that she drinks to wake her up. But a few moments later Gran stumbled up the stairs from her room in the basement into the kitchen and they both wished me a Happy Christmas! So, that was it. Today was Christmas! But it wasn't even snowing. After all that fuss and planning today was the day I got to find out what it was all about.

Mum and Gran got dressed and then put things out on the table for breakfast. They ate and talked about the fact it wasn't snowing or raining. They were always talking about the weather. Me, I just looked out the windows downstairs and saw if it was okay for me to go out or not. I didn't like getting my fur wet; I think I've mentioned that.

Then they went upstairs and one of them called me and kept calling but I wanted to go up really. I was curious to see what was going on. Hanging from one of the windows was a large stocking filled with presents for *me!* Another big sock lay next to it. I had two big presents and I didn't even wear socks!

Mum pulled the contents out of the big sock while I watched from a piece of wrapping paper - not my usual one but a new piece. This one had a softer, thicker feel. The sock was full of cat toys, Whiskas treats, cat nip mice and a little mouse all covered in glitter that jingled when I hit it with my paw. I'd also been given presents by my Auntie Gill (she'd seen me at the Home all those months ago). I had a fluffy mouse on a long string hanging from a rod. Mum had got me something similar only it was a furry thing but I had helped myself to that a few days earlier because Mum hadn't wrapped it. She had taken it away, wrapped it and put it back under the tree. I began to hit it with my paw. But then I saw the ball with the tasty Whiskas treats being rolled towards me. I hit that instead. Next a beautiful feeding dish was unwrapped and my eyes opened wide. I now had dozens, *hundreds*, of presents. Everything I touched with my paw sparkled, jingled or rattled when I touched it. And it was all for me. Anything else was edible - and I liked that even more. I'd even been given a new food bowl so I could eat my new treats from it. I just needed a little help opening packets and getting tops off. One of the big socks was from Auntie Jan and it was full of toys and a catnip mouse was at the bottom in the toe. I stared in amazement because the whole of the drawing room floor was covered in my toys, treats, presents and little amusements. People - friends of Mum's and mine had gone out and bought me things and I now had more presents than either Mum or Granny.

Mum had that stupid new camera that she used to take not very good photos and was taking snap after snap of me but this time I didn't mind. I felt really, really happy. But it wasn't over …

Gran handed Mum a big present. Her eyes were shining with anticipation and Mum's lit up when she saw it.

'Oh! What is it?' she asked.

Gran shook her head. 'Open it and see. It is really something for Kimmy as well.'

I couldn't fit any more presents on the paper I was sitting on. I was trying to decide which toy to play with next. I watched Mum as she pulled the paper off. Under the paper was some of that funny plastic paper with the bubbles. I decided to sit on that instead and I enjoyed the noise that each plastic bubble made as I pushed it with my paw. 'Bip … bip …'

'Oh Mum!' My Mum was talking to Gran and holding up something framed with wood. It was like one of the pictures she had on her walls - only this one looked more familiar than the usual one.

'It's Kimmy!' exclaimed Mum, 'You've had her portrait done'.

Gran smiled and nodded. 'Yes, do you like it?'

Mum's eyes had gone all moist and she was holding up the picture to look at closer. 'It's absolutely beautiful. I love it.'

She held it towards me and I looked at it closely. It was indeed a portrait of me and it really looked like me too. I didn't remember anyone making me pose for that but I was half asleep in it so maybe they had sneaked in when I wasn't looking. A moment later Mum had taken down the picture of an unknown cat by a famous artist, and hung my portrait in its place. I need to say that again. She hung *MY* portrait above the fireplace. An artist had painted me (from photos Gran said later) and he had got the likeness very good. It was me in my favourite position on the floor under the window. Well, having a portrait of oneself hanging above the fire in a big, old pink house with four floors; it doesn't get any posher does it? I even wondered if I was now an aristocrat. Or should I say an aristocat? I began to purr my approval.

'She looks pleased,' said Gran. And of course I was. For a second I wondered what presents Ginger was getting today - none probably. Instead of a gorgeous home cooked Christmas lunch, he was probably going to have the remains of something heated on a tray in the microwave. And he certainly wouldn't have his image immortalised on the wall forever and ever. But then I realised that I no longer cared about Ginger and what he did or anything at all about him. I'd been jealous of him for a while but now I had no need. I hoped he was well and happy because I had a wonderful Mum and a fantastic home. I loved the way that when Mum went out she brought me back something and when she was in she talked to me all the time. I just wished all the cats at Bath Cats and Dogs Home could find somewhere like this. There were hundreds of little cats - and dogs up there today not getting any presents or having a home of their own. It was clear that I was loved not just by my Mum but by her Mum too and Auntie Jan, Auntie Gill, Auntie Shirley, my pet feeder, Elaine from London, Sue, Mickey, Jamie, Porsche and Cassie and loads of other people (and *all* the cats from United Cats). I remembered how kind Jack and Louise had been to me all those weeks ago and how Jack was always asking after me. In the last six months I had gone from being an unwanted cat at Bath Cats and Dogs Home (although well looked after) into being the most wanted cat in the whole world. I thought of my two litter trays, my pop up timed box, the filtered water, my tent, the safe garden and all the cosy places I had to sleep. And now I had all the presents too.

I hauled myself into my favourite chair and settled myself down for a nap. My presents lay all around me. I would inspect them again later. Mum and Gran were pulling open *their* presents (mine had been opened first. That's how important I was!) and were throwing paper on the floor. They were making a terrible mess and I hoped they were going to clear it up. I had standards. And I also hoped they wouldn't throw my piece of paper out by mistake. Then Mum flicked the switch so that the fire in the grate came on. It was just like my dream way back at the Home! Me, in a comfy chair lying by the fire. And above me was my portrait. Later I would find a way to get the top off that tub of Whiskas treats but for now I was content to doze. I closed my eyes and sighed deeply and began to purr. I was happy - very happy and secure in a good home at last. And I went to sleep safe in the knowledge that I, Kimmy, had achieved my ultimate dream - to find a good home and be the most spoiled cat in Bath.

Top Tip

If your Mum isn't perfect straight away and doesn't spoil you enough - show her this book and she'll soon get the message.

CPSIA information can be obtained at www.ICGtesting.com
Printed in the USA
BVOW01s0912010816

457528BV00022B/146/P